Adventures in Healing

by

Steven Fanning

Adventures in Healing
© 2017 by Steven Fanning

Designed by Suzanne Austin Wells
Chauncey Park Press
735 N Grove Avenue
Oak Park, Illinois 60302
chauncey@wells1.com

Cover photo by Suzanne Austin Wells.
Monreale Cathedral, Sicily, 2016.

Printed in the United States of America
ISBN: 978-1548004354

Dedication

I saw that life is a precious gift from God and we should try to enjoy it. But life is also purposeful; it has meaning. The purpose of life is to learn and thus all that happens to us advances this purpose, even the worst things that happen to us.

—*Steven Fanning*

TABLE OF CONTENTS

PREFACE

This account of my illness and recovery is as accurate as I can make it although I have to admit that my memory is not absolutely reliable. Luckily I wrote down a detailed account of my hospital experiences in London and Chicago almost immediately after my discharge lest I lose those precious memories and I have been able to draw upon that document here. Also, I have been keeping a journal for many years, which I was able to cite to provide some of my immediate reactions to my experiences. Moreover, in my journals I recorded every event related to the healing work that I do, as they happened, which has proven to be invaluable for the precise and detailed account found in Chapter 6. The quotations taken from my initial written memories and from my journals are printed here in italics.

I could have written a more detailed and accurate version of my hospitalization in London if my brother Keith were still alive, but he died in 1994. I was in a coma or in a haze for the first three weeks of my stay at St. Bartholomew's

Hospital (commonly called Barts) in London, but both at the hospital at the time and over the following six years Keith and I had many conversations about my illness and my treatment at St. Bartholomew's and I have incorporated my best memories of what he told me into this report.

CHAPTER 1

An Unreal Reality

Often people have a rosy, romanticized view of what a Near Death Experience is like. The popular image is that after first soaring through a tunnel and emerging into magnificent light, you enter into a pastoral scene of stunning beauty. You might be greeted by an angel or perhaps Jesus, or maybe your deceased love ones. The entire atmosphere is one of peace and love. At some point you understand that you cannot remain in this idyllic paradise, but must return to your life on earth. After a reluctant return to your body, you no longer fear death or have even the slightest doubt about the reality of life after death. Who wouldn't want to experience such beauty, peace and assurance? It's almost as if an NDE would make a really great ride at a theme park.

Indeed sometimes this lovely scenario is entirely accurate, but often there is far more to the story. There are NDEs, in particular those that include the aspect known as the "life review," that present to people a very different view of themselves. They no longer are viewing themselves through rose-colored glasses manufactured by the ego, but instead they see themselves in the harsh, glaring light of supernal reality. Moreover, often experiencers are presented with an understanding of life and existence that is very much at odds with our common understandings of how things are. One's basic understanding of self and reality is shattered.

In addition, Near Death Experiences tend to come when one is near death. At times a number of difficult health problems remain after the NDE is over. In these cases, people have to work on rehabilitating their bodies in addition to trying to assimilate the "lessons" from the light into their lives. It may be an open question as to which is more difficult, physical rehabilitation or psychological and spiritual rehabilitation.

In such cases, the NDE is an earthquake that turns one inside out, demolishing one's basic understanding of God, self, life and the universe. The tremors and aftershocks continue on for years afterwards in the effort to integrate the lessons learned from the experience into life in this world. Moreover, people who have these experiences often find their own lives changed in ways that would have been unimaginable to them before the earthquake hit.

In this sense, an NDE can be much more than up the tunnel, into the paradise, and back into this world again. In such cases, the NDE is only the beginning of a long, difficult and challenging process of remaking one's very existence. Seen this way, what is commonly taken for an NDE only initiates the true, continuing Near Death Experience. After the return from what is beyond, the first and inescapable question is, "Now what?"

*　*　*

At the start of the summer of 1988, I am not sure that I had ever heard of a near-death experience, but as I began to come back into consciousness from a two-week coma in early July of that year, I was certain that I had had an experience, however it took me nine or ten days to understand that I had been perched on the brink of death while that experience unfolded.

The first week that I was out of the coma is wrapped in fog for me. I remember it only in the vaguest of scattered images. The fog that surrounded me would lift for a few very short moments, exposing a dimly perceived landscape, but then an impenetrable blanket of haze would settle back around me and obscure everything once more. Adding to the confusion were the bizarre and inconsistent images that confronted me. I would slowly emerge in the middle of one improbable reality, but then fade out of it, reawaken next in a different unbelievable world, only to descend into another cloud and reemerge into yet a different scene. It was not infinitely changing but rather there was a specific set of bizarre worlds into which I would slip in succession for brief periods, virtually rotating from one to another to another and back again.

One of the worlds that I was in was a hospital in a place that I didn't know, and I had no idea why I was a patient there. It seemed to be an international hospital, with people from England, Wales, Scotland, Ireland, Australia, New Zealand, the United States and India, whose origins were betrayed by the bewildering collection of accents that greeted me there. To make it worse, it seemed that I rarely saw the same face twice.

At the hospital was an odd assortment of people who did not belong together. In addition to the international mixture that was the hospital staff, my brother Keith, a park ranger in Oklahoma, was there, as was Majka, my friend who lived in Stockholm. I was perplexed—what could possibly account for their presence together at that place, for they did not know each other. Sometimes Keith and Majka would be there at the same time, but their joint appearance could just be my imagination, for other times Keith would be there alone while sometimes it would be just Majka.

But there was more confusion. For some reason, I didn't seem to be able move my arms or hold anything in my hands. My arms seemed to hang limply down at my sides. And then there was the pain, the unremitting pain that seemed to originate from deep inside my body and then radiate throughout my legs and feet, which were also unmovable. The pain was excruciating and unceasing. To compound the confusion and frustration, I could not speak. I moved my lips but no sound came out. I cried out, begging for help, but I was mute and no one understood what I was saying.

Sometimes music was playing, very near to me, over my head somewhere. It might be country music, with Willie Nelson or Waylon Jennings. Or it might be Barbra Streisand, or the Moody Blues, or classical music. There was no predicting or controling the selection.

At times I knew that my brother had a light blue Volkswagen Karmann-Ghia that turned into an airplane. I wanted to be away from the pain and confusion and I begged him to take me away from this place. But he never understood what I was saying and he never helped me.

That hospital was the scene of bizarre repeated events. At times it would seem that I would begin to regain feeling and movement but then, always at night when no one else was around, a physician would come into my room. He seemed to appear suddenly out of the darkness and jab a hypodermic needle into the underside of my upper arm, under my biceps. My whole arm would then go dead, filled with a hurting, tingling feeling. I wouldn't be able to feel anything or move my arm at all, and my body would then go numb and once again I could not move. By the next night, the pain would have diminished and I would be thinking that I might be able to move my arm. But then the same physician would reemerge from the darkness, repeat his torturous procedure and I would be paralyzed once more.

This same physician also presided over a gruesome procedure. A portable x-ray machine was brought into my room and the square x-ray film canister, hard and cold, was placed under my back. This physician then brought out some sort of tag on a string which he made me inhale into my lungs. But it wasnt placed quite right and he pulled the tag out of my lungs and made me do it again, and then a third time. It was an awful sensation as I inhaled that tag and the retrieval was just as ghastly as it seemed to rip at my lung tissue. I came both to hate and fear that doctor.

There was one wonderful and soothing recurring vision from that reality. I would be alone in a small room, but one much larger than the usual American hospital room. It would always be at night, with the room lit only by a dim, yellow glow so that I could just manage to make out what was around me. One of the nurses at the hospital, one of South African twins named de Boers, would be standing with her back to me. Then a bright, golden glow would burst out and fill the room, beaming out of something she was holding in front of her, out of my vision. She would turn to face me. The golden light was coming from a disk, perhaps four inches in diameter, making me think of a magical rice cake. She was grasping it with both hands held together, with thumbs facing herself while the index and second fingers were facing me. She extended the disk towards me, saying, "Do you want this? This is for you." Then she snapped the disk in half vertically and crumbled each half into several smaller pieces. She brought the pieces over to my bed and placed them into my respirator (although I had no idea why I should be on a respirator, I just was). Instantly the golden glow filled my body, infusing me with the most peaceful and contented feeling and I would drift off into the most wonderful, warm sleep. This was heavenly.

But there also were periodic frightening episodes. Across from me in my room was another patient, an African who had been mauled by a lion. At night, always at night, in the dim glow that permitted me to see just well enough to make out shapes, nurses would come into the room and go over to his bed. Then, in a horrifying scene, they would hover over him and cut off pieces of his body and stuff them into large transparent plastic bags. These they would then cram into a large cupboard by the windows to my right. I wondered if they would next turn their attention to me, but then the fog returned and I faded out of this ghastly scene.

Oddly, one of the physicians, the one who seemed to be in charge, I knew to be a former student of mine. I knew him well and told everyone so, but they just laughed at me. He was a specialist on communicable African diseases. Why was he working on me? I must have contracted some horrible disease, which explained why I was unable to move, but when and how could this have happened?

The physicians and nurses always seemed to be going out on weekend parties and, during the week, their lives seemed to consist of talking about the parties of the previous weekend and planning for those the one ahead. All of this seemed to be happening in Australia, but there many people in British military uniforms around. The name "Ponsonby" kept going through my head, seeming unrelated to anything, I just heard that name repeated over and over.

This world was not right. It could not be reality. I did have other worlds to pick from, however, but they were no more inviting than this one, yet at the same time most of them were no more bizarre.

Sometimes I was also at another hospital, a British military hospital that was located in an old estate house. I had been taken there in an ambulance that seemed to date from the 1940s -- long, white, windowless. I was also paralyzed in that hospital and needed the help of others in order to be shaved. An officer was always trying shave me to give me what he termed a "regimental look." He seemed not very good at it, especially when it came to my upper lip, and my face had dozens of nicks and cuts on it. People seemed preoccupied with shaving me. I wanted them not to try anymore, but instead to let the beard and moustache grow and spare my face the torturous cuts.

There was another place in which I also found myself, a world that, for a welcome change, I really enjoyed. It was in Minnesota, Wisconsin or some other place in the deep woods. I was lying in a bed in the kitchen of a house of a nurse, a very attractive nurse who seemed romantically interested in me and she usually tried to dress up to please me. The house, which was not in good repair, was surrounded by woods. It was summer--warm and sticky, and the cicadas in the trees were loud with their rhythmic buzz. The color yellow seemed to dominate a warm, dark, welcoming and very pleasant kitchen. I was still unable to move, even in this inviting place, and I just lay there while the nurse bustled around taking care of things there in the kitchen. While all this was going on, there was a radio playing in the background, a broadcast of a Minnesota Twins baseball game on WCCO radio in Minneapolis, announced in a voice that was somehow familiar to me. However, the game seemed never actually to be in progress at any time, but instead announcements of a contest were always coming over the radio.

At other times I was in San Francisco's Chinatown. I was lying on a mat, still unable to move. The room seemed to be something like an opium den, with dense smoke curling around, intertwining with everything as it pulled everyone into its embrace. There were many people there, all smoking some sort of pipe that was the source of the smoke, and they were also lying down, looking half asleep. One of the nurses from the strange, international hospital was there, one of the de Boer twins, only now she looked Chinese. There was much talk of Chinese astrology, with discussion about what name she should give to her son. She would come to me, place her hand on my chest and reassure me. "We will find something that will help you," she said in a voice that was deeply soothing. I drifted off into a haze.

Somehow associated with this scene was a different one related to Southeast Asia and attempts to find missing American prisoners of war and bodies. Again, drugs were involved, which served as bribes and payments to reach the desired destination. This was a very dangerous and frightening world.

In another world, I was lying on a sofa in a large department store. My eyes were closed but somehow I was looking down on the scene and could see what was happening. I was on some sort of television screen so I could see myself lying there on the sofa. I had a very sleepy look on my face, but I was smiling. Majka, my friend from Sweden, was with me, as were two women speaking in British accents (one of them looked like Jean Marsh, who played Rose on the BBC series *Upstairs, Downstairs*), who were supposed to be nurses. However, they were mostly fascinated with watching themselves on the television screen. That television seemed to be a two-way communicator, for there was a voice coming out of it, the voice of my former student, the physician from the reality of the international hospital. The voice told me over and over again, "Steven, wake up, you have suffered an asthma attack, you are in London." However, the scene looked nothing like London or a hospital and I could never wake up.

There was another completely different and very complicated scene. It seemed to be a Mexican restaurant set in some desert place with nearby mountains, such as New Mexico. In the center of the restaurant was a large decorative pool with a shipwreck in its middle which had sharks circling around it. At the restaurant the food was good, especially the bread and the salads. However, all of this was a front for a gambling racket that kept the patrons in the debt of the owner, a man who resembled Ricardo Montalban. My brother was there, too, but he had fallen into their trap. I tried to warn him, to free him from their grasp, but he refused to listen. I also had my own reason for wanting to get away. I felt that I was being injected with something called shark venom, which had paralyzed me, and if I could get away from there and go back home, toxicological tests could be run, the exact nature of the venom discovered and I could be cured. I wanted Keith to take his flying Karmann-Ghia and fly me away from the restaurant, but he, being completely taken in by the scheme, didn't want to leave. I tried to taunt him into leaving by ridiculing his ability to fly the car but it had no effect.

In yet a different world, I was in the U. S. South, perhaps deep in rural northern Louisiana. The details are unclear to me, but it was also a very complicated scene, involving drugs, poisons, strange flowers and money left to someone's descendants.

None of these weird worlds could possibly be real. But what was worse, I knew no way of determining what was genuine from what was an hallucination or a dream, for I was no one. I had no past. I did not know who I was or how I came to be in any of these places. Of course I knew who Keith and Majka were, but they were in a very improbable scene, and still I was no one. How could I possibly judge which, if any, of these worlds was the real one? Possibly they all were real or maybe none was, for none of those worlds seemed very real, but they all were shadowy, lacking substance or reality. To make everything worse, I would be in one of these scenes only to have it fade out and then I would slowly reemerge in another one, only for it to fade out in its turn as I slipped into yet a different world. Always it was the same set of scenes, but none of them were present for very long.

In time, the international hospital seemed to be present more often than the other worlds. I don't know what happened to those other worlds I had been in, but eventually I seemed to be lodged firmly in this one, as unreal as it was. I remember my brother standing over my bed, speaking to one of the physicians, telling him it was the Fourth of July back home. There was a terrible heatwave and the water level of the Mississippi river had fallen so much that barges were stranded.

But even as this improbable reality came to dominate, it was still too bizarre to accept. I was alone in the room, but usually I could see no other patients except for the one in the opposite bed, the African mauled by the lion. It looked like no hospital room that I had ever seen, appearing to be more of a storage room. I could not move my arms or legs or hold objects in my hands although people kept putting things into them which I was expected to hold, even though I couldn't. I could only see clearly a few feet beyond my bed and beyond that range everything was a blur. What was wrong with my eyes? I could not make sounds when I tried to speak although I could form words with my mouth. But it didn't matter, for only occasionally could anyone read my lips. Even a microphone that was brought in to be placed against my throat, thus amplifying the sound, was useless. However, sometimes the people there could read my lips which, along with gestures, there was some very limited communication. And there was the pain, the never-ending pain that seemed to emanate from the very core of my feet. Moreover, my head was heavy, incredibly heavy, and it would list over to one side and it was almost impossible for me to lift it back to an upright position again.

This was no world that I recognized or wanted to be in. I looked up at some medical equipment over the head of my bed. The writing was in English and French. Why French? My brother told me that I was in London. I refused to believe him for I had no memory of being in London (and why was the writing in French, and what about all those non-English accents that I was hearing?) He asked me where I thought I was. I told him either Paris or Oak Park (Illinois). He looked at me as though I were an amusing child and laughed.

There was some metal object pressing against the septum of my nose while something else was tied tightly around my right ear, neither of which could I see. The pressure caused tremendous pain to both nose and ear and, whatever those things were, I wanted them off in the worst way. Periodically whatever was tied to my ear would loosen, which brought great relief to both my ear and my nose. But then the nurses, especially a young nurse from India, would come in and tighten it again and the pain would return with all its fury. I hated it and resented her. This was nothing but torture.

Somehow over several days a vague understanding of this strange world had come to me. I believed that I had been kidnaped by these people and they had brought me here in that old ambulance. They injected me with paralyzing agents and the physician would reinject me with something each night to keep me paralyzed. I would be like this forever if I ever gave in and accepted the situation, thus I had to resist in order to have any chance at escape. I wanted my brother to fly me away in his Karmann-Ghia to our mother's house where I would get better. But no matter how I tried to tell him this, he never understood what I was trying to say. It was so damned frustrating.

However, I could resist with my limited means. If I ever gave in and accepted all this, I would be doomed to remain paralyzed, thus when the Indian nurse came to tighten whatever it was that was on my ear and nose, I would wiggle my head around, making it difficult for her to pull it tightly and restore the pain to my nose and ear. "Oh, Steve, you are impossible!" she shouted once, looking extremely irritated with me. That made me smile for I had won a tiny little victory. I did not know what was on my ear, but I imagined a little spiraling ribbon hanging down from it, which had been put there to punish me for being so bad. But I had company. There were times when I saw Queen Victoria in my room, up above me, close to the ceiling. She had a great number of white, spiraling ribbons hanging from her hair. I thought that she must have been very bad to have earned so many of them.

But the pain, especially in my feet, seemed to be the worst affliction. It was unbearable and unending. Nothing seemed to help. There were times when I would look down at my feet and I saw no skin covering them, just the raw, exposed tissues, looking like sausages wrapped around the bones of my feet. They were such painful sausages and there seemed to be no relief from their pain. I would ask Majka to rub my feet, for that did ease the pain somewhat, and she would massage them for as long as she could. The only other partial relief that I could count on was changing the position my legs were in. I came to love having my legs be moved into a "frog" position, with the heels being drawn up together, my knees pointed out to the side. This gave me some temporary ease from the constant pain and I loved it.

However, the pain was still incessant and no medicines seemed to help very much. I had to find some way to deal with it. Somewhere, now deep in my own past that I no could no longer remember clearly, I had read that resistance to pain, fighting the pain, only made it worse. One should love the pain, embrace it. Feeling desperate, I decided that it was worth giving it a try. I concentrated on loving the pain, trying to take it into myself, to make it a very part of me as if it belonged in me. Strangely the pain diminished, moving closer to a bearable level, at least for a while. What a surprise!

I came to understand that paralysis and numbness were two different things. Previously I think that I would have understood that paralysis meant that at least there would be no pain. But there are many different sets of nerves in the body, from those of the skin that tell us we have brushed against something to those that allow us to move our muscles to the deep trunk nerves. Just because those that allow for muscle movement are not working properly, it does not thereby mean that others, the ones that send pain signals, are also not functioning. It was clear to me that those pain nerves were in fine shape, doing their appointed job very well.

I was in a consistent world but still not in a comfortable one. Bizarre features persisted. There was a small television in my room, which I hated but the nurses seemed to like, so I didn't complain. It was Wimbledon season and tennis was on, seemingly without end. There was news, but it was unbelievable and did nothing to make me feel like this was where I belonged. The United States Navy had shot down an Iranian airliner and several hundred people had died, but that seemed impossible, for my country would never do such a thing. And there was a fire on an offshore oil rig named Piper Alpha, whatever that was supposed to mean, and there were people on television with horrible burns. There was no familiarity to this dark and ominous world.

One of the more irritating features of this place was a stream of people coming into my room, nearly always with very large smiles on their faces. These people, complete strangers to me, all behaved the same way. They would come over, smile at me as if they knew me very well, sometimes reach out and pat or touch me, and say something like, "You dont know how lucky you are to be alive."

I didn't understand. Lucky? Being trapped in this insane asylum in excruciating pain, unable to move or to talk very much at all, being tortured? "Try being in my place," I kept thinking, "and you won't feel so lucky."

In time the other worlds ceased to intrude into my consciousness. I did, however, miss that warm, yellow kitchen in the house in the woods, for I was stuck at the international hospital where they had kidnaped and drugged me into paralysis. This was the only reality for me now, whether it made sense or not. It was the second week out of the coma, but for me it was the first week that I can recall with any coherence, and I was utterly miserable. All I could think about was somehow getting out of there and returning home, wherever that might be. And then there was still the constant pain.

One night in the early part of this second week, my former student who seemed to be in charge of me came and asked me if I would like to talk. I said yes. He put something down my throat and there was the sound of metal on metal. Something tightened in my throat, choking me. It was awful. But then something gave way and a metal ring was removed from my throat, and at last my vocal chords could make sounds. They were not pleasant sounds, but I could croak out words. At last I could speak.

My former student turned out not to be Dr. Charles Hinds, president of the European Intensive Care Association, and he told me that I had suffered an asthma attack, that I was in St. Bartholomew's Hospital (commonly just called Barts) in London, and that indeed I was paralyzed. Thinking of all the pain that had been inflicted on me by his band of torturers and kidnappers, I told him that I did not trust him or anyone else at that hospital, and that I wanted to go home. With great kindness in his voice, he told me that he would do everything he could to get me home. At last there was hope.

Soon my head began to clear and I came to understand my situation. At the time I could not remember how I got to London, but slowly fragments of memories came together with what I was told later by the hospital staff, Majka and my brother to form a coherent story. I had been invited to give a scholarly talk in London and some friends of mine who lived in England had asked me to come and stay with them the week before the talk. In a sense the trip was destined not to go well. After I had bought my airline tickets, my friends canceled their invitation, citing vague difficulties that it would cause them. It wasn't clear why these difficulties weren't apparent before they extended the invitation and now I was left with no place to be for the first week of my working vacation. So I decided to go to Sweden to visit Majka. Overall it was a pleasant week, for I enjoyed seeing her after several years and together we visited several Viking-age sites that I was interested in seeing, such as Birka and Old Uppsala, because I taught a course on the history of the Vikings. Not all went smoothly, however, for Majka's boyfriend John was rather unreasonably jealous of my presence in Stockholm and especially incensed that I was staying at Majka's flat while she stayed with him and he made our spending time together as difficult as possible. I had lots of time to spend on my own, wandering the streets of the Old City of Stockholm and going to museums. On my last night in Stockholm, Majka and I were settling down to a bowl of soup and last minute conversation when John called and announced that he was coming over to her flat. Quickly I had to leave. I swept up my belongings and took a late train over to the apartment of Majka's friend Iwona, who generously took me in as a refugee that night.

The next morning I took a flight to England so that I could present my talk on the following day. However, the air quality was poor in London when I arrived and warnings had been issued urging those with pulmonary problems to avoid going out of doors, but, being on holiday and not checking news broadcasts regularly, I was completely unaware of them. I took a bus to Greenwich to see an exhibit commemorating the four-hundredth anniversary of the English victory over the Spanish Armada. But as the day wore on, I began to have trouble with my asthma, which had been a chronically severe problem for me for the past few years.

From this point on, my memory of events is very faulty, but apparently my asthma worsened and soon I was in a full medical crisis with a severe asthma attack. Paramedics were called and early on the morning of June 15, 1988, they took me to the emergency room at St. Bartholomew's Hospital where quickly my conditioned deteriorated to the point that I was in pulmonary arrest and was placed on a respirator. For a week my lungs were scarcely functioning. I had been given the highest possible levels of every bronchial dilator that might work to open my lungs, but they were ineffective. At times the blockage in my lungs was so severe that the respirator would shut down. I was alive now only because the hospital staff had "bagged me" by hand, squeezing away on the manual respirator to keep air moving into my lungs and bloodstream. At last, after a week, my lungs began to function but then I had a very high, life-threatening fever and had severe diarrhea. I had been wrapped in damp cloths to help bring down the fever. At the end of another week, the fever broke. I was out of the coma, but I suffered some sort of seizure and a spinal tap and CAT scan were performed on me in an effort to discover the cause.

And then the medical staff noted that I was making "no spontaneous movement." At first it was assumed that

I was suffering from Guillain-Barré Syndrome, a well-known illness resulting from damage to the nerve sheaths, which usually means a recovery period of six months to two years. But then an EMG (electro-myograph, a test of nerve conductivity) was done on me and it was discovered that matters were more serious, for the damage was to the nerve fibers, not the sheaths. This was entirely different. I was told that I might recover in two years, but the most likely prognosis was this would be a permanent paralysis.

What was the cause of the paralysis? It was never discovered even though, as I was told at St. Bartholomew's, they had "cultured everything there was to culture," and the CAT scan and a spinal tap had been performed. I was told that there were three possible causes of the paralysis. It could have been due to anoxia, my being on such low levels of oxygen for such a long period of time because of pulmonary arrest, or it might have been the result of the very high levels of all the medicines they had given me in an effort to get my lungs working again, not to mention the six or seven different antibiotics I had also been given when my fever was raging. The third alternative was that it was some unknown agent, bacterial or viral, that had somehow got into my system. When I had been in Stockholm I had fallen into Lake Mälaren and scraped my leg in the process. Perhaps that was the cause. In the end the "diagnosis" was really just a description of my condition: peripheral polyneuropathy, which meant simply that my arms and legs were paralyzed. What baffled the hospital staff was that they could find almost no other examples in medical literature of this sort of condition. I was a medical mystery and we were all in very new territory.

The paralysis, however, was very selective. If asked to pull in my arms or legs, I could do nothing. But if my arms or legs were moved up close to my body, I could push out with amazing strength, almost knocking down whoever was holding them. It was the retractor muscles that were paralyzed, not the extenders. But once my arms and legs had extended, I was powerless to move them any more. It's hard to describe what my paralysis was like. The pain aside, my arms and legs didn't feel especially different. In my hands, arms and legs for the most part, I had normal ability to feel at skin level. It wasn't like getting anesthesia at the dentist's, when the mouth, tongue and lips go dead and you have trouble talking or spitting. My feet, however, were a different matter, for they were largely numb as well as paralyzed. Moreover, when I wanted to move, to reach, to grab, nothing happened. My mind was busy sending signals, but there just was no response. I would look at my unresponsive arms and hands and, in my head, say to them, "What's up? Move!"

I quickly learned one of the most basic lessons in paralysis -- give up all ideas of modesty. I couldn't feed myself, brush my own teeth, wash myself or wipe myself off. I couldn't close a pajama fly that was gaping open. I was catheterized and the tubing needed tending to from time to time. I decided that there was absolutely nothing that I could do about it and there was nothing to be gained by fretting about it. That's just the way it was and I had to live with it.

There was another disturbing consequence of my illness. I had almost no muscle mass remaining. I looked down at my body and it was unrecognizable, nothing but a bony skeleton. I had lost perhaps sixty pounds and now I might weigh in at around 135 pounds. Since I had stood 6' 2" tall, there really wasn't very much to me. At some point in the second week of my consciousness, the fourth week of the illness, I was asked if I would like to see what I looked like. Of course I did and a mirror was brought over. I was astonished. My face was thin, even gaunt, not at all familiar to me. Also, after more than three weeks in the ICU, my hair was a mess, gummed up with the residue of glue from the EEG electrodes.

One of the consequences of the entire episode was fairly severe memory loss. I still could not remember going to England, and the asthma attack that had led to all this damage was totally unknown to me. In general, my memory was very spotty. I did remember having two children. When asked their ages, I didn't know. Somehow I knew that my son was born in 1973 and that this was 1988, so I said fifteen. I thought that my daughter was three years younger than he (she is four and a half years younger), so I said twelve (she was ten).

At one point, I complained to Hazel Havley, an ICU nurse from Wales, letting her know how upset I was that no one would talk to me about my condition or ask me what I wanted done to me. She responded with a big laugh, "Steve, we do talk to you about it, but you can't remember a damned thing!" I did remember those words of Hazel, however.

So, I was paralyzed. I could move nothing below my neck, and my head was impossibly heavy and seemed to be hanging off to one side. Jokingly I asked Maura Falvey (this was one of the de Boers twins from my bizarre visions--there was only one of her and she was a nurse from Ireland, not South Africa), if they had filled my head with lead.

My brother was concerned that I was giving up all resolve to fight to improve my condition. As I came back into consciousness, I was telling him that I was no good, that they might as well just throw me away. Keith became very upset and began giving me pep talks, throwing sports clichés at me, "When the going gets tough, the tough get going," that sort of thing. He was really getting on my nerves, for he didn't understand at all. I mouthed a few words. He didn't understand and asked, "What?" He leaned closer. I repeated it. He looked stunned and said, "Did you just call me an asshole?" I smiled and thought, "Ah, how I love communication."

However, as my mind cleared, I didn't find my condition entirely distressing. I truly did wonder how I would ever make a living. Could I go back to my university teaching career? I supposed that I could get around in a wheelchair and still lecture, if my voice ever recovered. I didn't feel overwhelmed by the paralysis, but I was indeed very concerned about the mechanics of living as a quadriplegic. The reason was that, while I had been in the coma, I had been away having a secret experience, known only to me. As a result, I knew that whatever the future, it would somehow be OK. But I also knew that indeed I was worthless. That judgment was not the product of pain or depression, it was simply the truth. That private experience had truly given me an entirely new perspective on myself.

CHAPTER 2.

In a Place Beyond[1*]

I don't know at what point in my two-week coma I had my experience and I have no doubt that there was more to my experience than I can remember, for the memory loss that resulted from my illness was severe. However, the memories that I do have are vivid and unforgettable and they changed my life. Moreover, to describe the experience in some sort of sequential form is to distort it. There was no time where I was and I learned that time is a necessary convenient fiction for this world, but it did not exist in that one. Everything seemed to be at one moment, even when "events" seemed to occur one after the other.

The reality that I was in was more real, more intense, than anything in this current world of ours. It was Hyper-Reality. I was in a place surrounded by flatness and barrenness. What seemed to be the sky, the land and

---

[1*]More than ten years after my illness I met the renowned philosopher of religion Huston Smith, best known for his classic *The World's Religions*. He was interested in my experience and I provided him with a preliminary draft of the first part of this chapter. He then used much of that account in his Ingersoll Lecture, "Initimations of Immortality," for 2001-02 at Harvard University. That lecture appears in the *Harvard Divinity Bulletin* 30:3 (Winter 2001-02), pp. 12-15, and I am grateful to Huston for providing me with a copy.

everything, was a pale blue-grey color. It was like being on a raft in the middle of the ocean where sky and sea merge into one monochromatic world, but I felt as though I were standing on firm land. The blue-grey vastness seemed to stretch out endlessly in all directions.

Beside me was a Being, whom I never saw but whose presence I felt constantly. I felt the Being's constant enormous, powerful presence.

With the Being beside me, exuding love and comfort to me, I re-experienced my life in a way that was not what I would have expected. As I was growing up in a fundamentalist Christian church, I had been told many times about what it would be like when one faced God after death. It would be something like watching God's movie of your life (as in Albert Brooks' film *Defending Your Life*). There would be all the scenes of your life. You would watch them on the screen and there would be little that you could do other than admit to the actions that were so clearly recorded there. "Well, I guess you got me, fair and square." But this is not how it was. What happened to me was a *re-experiencing* of my life, but from three different perspectives *simultaneously*.

One perspective was my version of my life as I might have recounted it to anyone patient enough to listen. However, it was not a re-living of events but rather a re-living *and* re-experiencing of the *emotions, feelings* and *thoughts* of my life. Here were the emotions that I had felt and why I had believed that I had them. Here were my conscious reasons for the actions that I had taken. Here were the hurts I felt and my responses to them. Here was my emotional life as I recalled having experienced it. I can now remember only the most important events of my life and if the re-living involved every single event of my life, not all of it survived in my memory.

However, at exactly the same time as I was re-experiencing *my* version of my life, I was also experiencing my life from the perspective of those with whom I was involved. I now felt what they felt, I lived their emotions as they acted with and reacted to me. This was *their* version of *my* life. When I thought they were clearly out of line and reacted with anger or thoughtlessness, I experienced their pain and frustration. I felt the effects and consequences of my actions. This was an absolutely different view of my life and it was not a pretty one. It was shocking to feel the pain that another person experienced because of what I had done, even as, when I acted, I believed myself to have been fully justified because of that person's own actions. I told myself that I was justified in what I did, but their pain was real. It hurt.

In addition, however, also at exactly the same time, I experienced a *third* view of my life. It was not my version, with my justifications. It was not that of the others in my life, with their version of my life and their own justifications for their own actions, thoughts and feelings. It was an unbiased view, free of the subjective and self-serving rationalizations that I and others had used to support the countless acts of selfishness and lack of true love in our lives. To me, it can only be described as God's view of my life. It was what had *really* happened, the real motivations. Stripped away were my lies to myself, lies that I actually believed, my self-justification, my preference to see myself always in the best light.

I did not find myself in hell but I was suffering

torment. It was horribly painful to experience the fullness of my life and I was filled with contempt for myself. How could I have been so incredibly stupid as to believe my own lies? In particular it hurt to discover that I had been hiding behind my version of logic in order to deny emotional truths.

All of this—the three-way re-experiencing of my life and the self-judgment—was simultaneous and yet separate and distinct. There was no such thing as the sequence of events that we believe to be the essence of time.

In the end, I heard a judgment on my life, but the judgment came from me, it was my own judgment of myself. It came from within me and it had my voice. My life was clear to me. I was a failure. I was not who I thought I was, I was not who I could be.

And through all this the Being was at my side. I felt nothing but love and support from the Being. It exuded emotion: you are loved, you are lovable; your worst fault is that you are human. It goes with the territory. I remember the words, "Don't worry, you're only human."

However, I was in emotional agony. It was terrible to know that I was a mere mortal, just like everyone else, for I had thought that I was so much better than that. But the Being accepted me. The Being was letting me know that it was not acceptable to hurt other people, but it is part of the human condition. It's not alright, but it's alright.

Next, if I can really talk about a next, in that Hyper-Reality where time and sequence do not really exist, I felt that I was given an understanding of everything that is, at least everything that is really important. I felt as if all the secrets of the universe were revealed to me -- not mathematical formulas, but simply how the universe operates, what is true, how things are. I now knew everything.

I was given an understanding of my own family, of why everyone was the way that they were and I fully comprehended the dynamics of my family. At last I understood completely who I was and why I was the person that I was. Previously I had a great deal of anger at my parents for what I believed their failings to have been, for the pain I believed they had caused me. Now I understood and it was so simple. They were flawed human beings, struggling with their own problems, doing their best under those circumstances. I now knew so very well that certainly they were no worse than I had seen myself to have been. Their human failings didn't matter any more.

I also came to understand the purposefulness of life. Everything that had happened to me, even the worse things, were necessary. I didn't understand the exact reason for every single event in my life, but I understood that life is about learning and growing, and those pains were necessary. I no longer resented them.

I also understood the utter simplicity of life. What is true is simple, stunningly simple. I saw that any explanation that is complicated and convoluted is probably false. A good starting place for understanding truth could well be to read Robert Fulghum's *All I Really Need to Know I Learned in Kindergarten*. The Rules of Life really are simple and straightforward. A couple of years later I read Julian of Norwich's *Showings*, and in that work she stated that God showed her all that was, and it was no bigger than a hazelnut in the palm of her hand. It reminded me of what I had been shown, all that is important is really so small and so simple. It is what we all really already know in our hearts. And now I knew all this with an understanding that is beyond knowing. I felt the force of those truths.

I saw that life is a precious gift from God and we should try to enjoy it. But life is also purposeful, it has meaning. The purpose of life is to learn and thus all that happens to us advances this purpose, even the worst things that happen to us. As much as I dislike trying to create coherent and consistent systems, if I were to try to explain what life is all about, based on the pieces that I feel were revealed to me, it would be this—all of life has a purpose. I suspect that whoever we really are, not our selves as we think of our selves (this jumps into cosmology with the existence of our selves already established, and I can't speculate on the origin of our selves), we choose to come into our current incarnations, even making decisions on the exact circumstances (parents and living conditions) into which we are born because we think that those circumstances will provide us with the proper opportunities to grow as entities in the way that each of us needs to grow. That is, the challenges that we face in our lives are intentional and purposeful.

We can indeed face these challenges and deal with them as we meet them in our lives or we can refuse to do so and we can run away from them. But we can never escape them and we will continue having to encounter them in our lives until we do face them and grow through that very experience, or until we die. It seems to me that if we die without having successfully faced those challenges, we will just have to come back in another incarnation and try again. Therefore the very essence of our lives is the challenge that life presents us, which is not an intrusion but rather the very reason why we are alive.

I can imagine a scenario in which, before our incarnation, we find a really good challenging set of circumstances which, if met successfully, will allow us to make rapid progress in growing as entities. Then, upon becoming incarnate, we find that we have bitten off more than we can chew and we find that the challenge is too great, life is too hard, and we retreat from it. Being alive in this world is very challenging for our selves, with so many pleasures, side lanes and distractions, and opportunities to fail to meet our self-imposed challenges. If we do not meet our challenges successfully, we are not failures because the challenges are very great, but we do fail to grow as we really want to.

I can't even imagine a convincing scenario to explain the whole picture -- the nature of our selves, why our selves need to grow in the first place. But I feel very sure about the purpose and meaning of life being to grow as selves and that the challenges that we face are necessary and purposeful.

The revelations given to me contained nothing directly concerning reincarnation, but I can accept it as being consistent with what was given to me and with my own conjectures, as just described. However, I don't believe that any system of thought concerning reincarnation is correct, for it just doesn't seem right. I saw that there was no me that I would recognize as me. We usually identify our habits as ourselves, but that is false. There is no bundle of habits and behaviors that gets passed from body to body in successive incarnations, so we have no reason to identify ourselves with any particular past life, for that "person" is not us, but living in a different time, space and physical body. Our selves are not what we think they are.

Because life is a precious gift, it became clear to me that the worst thing we can do is to kill another person, for life is not ours to take. The second worst thing is to kill ourselves, for the same reason. Suicide is a sign that we have failed to learn what we need to learn, that we have given up the life that was given us. Accordingly, capital punishment is wrong, for it is the conscious, intentional taking of life, which is never OK, in the name of vengeance, the worst excuse for any action. To be true to our own genuine nature, we should love people, be kind to people, do no harm. I understood that it is never OK intentionally to hurt another person. We can't control other people so we can't live in such a way that another person will not feel pain because of our actions, but that is not our responsibility. Our responsibility is not to intend to cause pain to others and to be conscious of their feelings and emotions.

In addition, I understood that there is no sin in the traditional sense. The wrong or harmful things that we do mostly harm ourselves. We can't offend God. While we can do many things that are simply wrong, they are not an offense to a higher power, they simply represent us being humans and doing what humans do. We are only human and making errors is what humans do, as is being thickheaded and stubborn. We do make mistakes but it isn't OK, for we are to learn how not to make those mistakes, which is one of the principal purposes of life. We should not be complaisant about our mistakes nor should they be accepted as being alright, but most of the harm that is done is done to ourselves as we let ourselves down and fail ourselves.

I was then in the middle of the universe, like the space baby at the end of the movie *2001*. Around me in all directions were innumerable stars, clusters, nebulae and galaxies, blazing with light and arrayed in three-dimensional glory. It was breathtakingly beautiful. Space stretched out in all directions and continued on forever and, what is more, I felt rays of connection tying me directly to all that I saw, to each and every object. I was an integral part of the universe. It was where I belong and everything in the universe is connected to everything else.

Then I was shown scenes of the future. What I remember especially concerned my children. They would have serious problems with their mother and they would need me. I also saw scenes of my future life, vague pictures of me in a church and with people that I did not then know. In time, all of these visions of future events did in fact occur.

I remember making a positive decision. I wanted to come back to life. I wanted to do what I would be needed for. I then began my slow climb out of the coma and into consciousness. And then I began waking up to the confusing worlds of the international hospital, the military hospital, the San Francisco opium den, the kitchen in the house in the woods. When the consistent reality of St. Bartholomew's hospital came to dominate and I came to understand that I was a quadriplegic, I was not frightened, but I certainly was concerned. I did not believe that there was a God, I *knew* it beyond any kind of mental assent. I knew that whatever happened, it would be alright. Of course no one else was aware of what I had experienced and there was no way that I could describe it all. It truly was ineffable.

* * *

Nothing in my religious past prepared me for this experience. My religious foundations were laid as I was raised in a fundamentalist church (the Church of Christ) in Oklahoma and West Texas. My family had always been very active members of the church, and if the church doors were open, we were there, attending services on Sunday morning, Sunday evening and Wednesday evening, and during summers we always were there for revivals and of course, Vacation Bible School. The chief tenets of the Church of Christ are Biblical literalism and the belief in the sole authority of the New Testament in religious matters. If the New Testament says do something, it should be done, and if one can't find a New Testament passage that says something should be done, then it should not be done. This policy translates into the church motto, "Speak where the Bible speaks and be silent where the Bible is silent." For example, because there is no mention in the New Testament of musical instruments in the church, they should not be there, and the same is true for choirs as well, thus only a capella singing by the entire congregation is permitted.

I was taught a very clear view of religion. God laid down the rules and they must be followed or else the punishment that is promised will be imposed. Do it or else. Religion was all in the head, consisting of learning the rules and following them and any form of emotional religion was disdained. Pentecostals who speak in tongues and claim to experience the Holy Spirit were dismissed as Holy Rollers, and purported visions of God, saints or angels were laughed off. God was a sane and rational god, certainly not one associated with hysterics.

In the view of religion that I was taught, those who followed the rules did not sin, and when such people died, they would go to Heaven. Those who disobeyed a rule, any rule, no matter how small, sinned and when they died they would go to their eternal punishment in Hell. Of course no human was perfect, but if you acknowledged sins, sincerely repented of them and genuinely intended not to repeat them, you would be forgiven and restored to a state of grace, until the next sin. And so the cycle repeated. You were either in a state of grace or in a state of sin, and the state you were in could change in an instant, over and over again endlessly. It was not quite like the fourth- and fifth-century heresy of Pelagianism, for it was not believed that humans could lead a life, on their own goodness, that merited Heaven, because all sinned. But God had created the mechanism of confession and repentance that made up for human failings. It was harsh but straightforward, but God made the rules and that was that. (Once I learned that Kenneth Starr, the leader of the Whitewater special counsel investigation against Bill and Hillary Clinton, was a member of the Church of Christ, I understood his grim determination to make them pay for what he considered to be their sins. The God of the Church of Christ is a god of justice, not mercy.) Simply wanting to do good was not good enough. When people died, they would go before God and be judged on the basis of what they had done and how recently they had been pardoned for their sins. God would make the decision and either Heaven or Hell awaited. Sin was an unfortunate reality but it was our own fault.

As a boy I had flourished in the Church of Christ. I

was usually a standout in Sunday School, for biblical history seemed easy for me to learn and I truly enjoyed it. Soon I was being groomed to be a preacher. As a sophomore in high school, on the long bus trips travelling to basketball games, often some distance away, a few of the other players on the team (mostly Baptists) and I fell into religious disputation and soon it was me against the Baptists. It was exhilarating. I even typed up written tracts amplifying on my views, fully documented with biblical citations, as I attempted to refute Baptist beliefs. By my junior year of high school, the momentum of my life in the Church of Christ had carried me forward to the point that I had even started preaching, but at the same time I was in the process of apostatizing.

I began my fall over the issues of dancing and drinking, both of which were considered grave sins in the Church of Christ. I had started dancing at parties in junior high, careful to conceal it from my parents and resorting to lies when they asked me if I danced. I took my first drink of alcohol as a sophomore in high school, an awful beer and Coke concoction given me by a friend at a drive-in movie theater just outside the city limits of Childress, Texas.

In my mind, I was not violating the creed of the Church of Christ, "Speak where the Bible speaks and be silent where the Bible is silent." The New Testament did not specifically condemn dancing and I found the proof texts that condemn revelry unconvincing when they were interpreted as referring to dancing. While drunkenness is often condemned in the New Testament, drinking itself is not and, after all, Jesus had made pretty good wine out of jugs of water. I argued that the New Testament also condemned gluttony and when was the last sermon anyone had ever heard in which a preacher condemned overeating? It seemed to me that the Church of Christ was being awfully selective when it came to the condemnation of sin.

I began arguing my points in Sunday School, exasperating the teacher. Soon he gave up and the preacher himself came in to take over the unruly class, which meant me. I kept up my refrain, "Speak where the Bible speaks, etc.," giving no ground on my insistence on consistency. In my mind I was the one upholding genuine Church of Christ teachings and fighting hypocrisy. I insisted on having a panel discussion on the questions of dancing and drinking. Soon the preacher wouldn't speak to me or shake my hand, nor would his wife, the elders of the church or their wives. Things were accelerating out of control in a hurry.

At the same time, a religious war was also breaking out at home. My dad was a pharmacist and science had always been valued in our family. Then a chatter of concern arose at the church over evolution, but to me there was no trouble with evolution, for I had been reading about Theistic Evolution, the concept that evolution was directed by God. Thus I saw no necessary conflict between religion and science. But then, in that same momentous junior year of high school, there was a petition at the church, urging the Texas Textbook Commission not to approve for adoption in Texas schools any biology textbook that did not view evolution as a crack-pot theory and creationism as the proper understanding of biology. To my horror I saw my mother walking down the central aisle of the church to sign the petition. When we got home from church I chewed her out for caving in to small-mindedness. She argued back on the basis of a literal interpretation of the first chapters of Genesis, while I responded with a more poetic interpretation, that the "days" of creation could refer to any length of time, and besides, how could the "days" be anything like we think of when the sun wasn't even created until the fourth "day"? My dad, a very religious man, didn't care for my attack on Biblical literalism or on an activity undertaken at the church. He joined in on Mother's side and matters and tempers escalated and soon virtually every Sunday afternoon after church was taken up with our arguments over evolution and creationism. Before long, my brother and his wife joined in against me as well. It was me against all of them, which in a perverse way I loved, for I felt that I was in my natural element, being the lone advocate of truth in the face of my enemies.

For more than a year, the religious war raged. Each issue was thoroughly dissected as we plowed through the fine points of every conceivable strand of the debate. At last we had come down to the basic difference: either one believed in the literal interpretation of Genesis and the world was created in six twenty-four hour days and it could be only about 6000 years old, or else Genesis was not literally true and some sort of evolution, perhaps directed by God, was possible.

In the end, pushed either to affirm or reject the literalness of the Bible, my dad took his stand, looked at me defiantly and announced, "I believe that the world was created in six twenty-four-hour days."

The matter was now closed and my faith in him was crushed, for I believed that he had sold out his mind for a position that I thought was utter rubbish. At the same time, I felt a twinge of guilt, for I felt that he never would have taken that ridiculous stand if I had not pushed him to decide between the Bible and science. That was the end of our debates, but it also shattered my last attachment to the Church of Christ, already badly frayed over the debates over dancing and drinking. I had decided that it was hypocritical, not adhering to its own beliefs, and it could not possibly be the one true church as it claimed to be.

Shifting my thinking only slightly, now I needed to find the *real* one true church. I was dating a Catholic and I had been attending church with her as often as I could without pushing my parents over the brink (the Church of Christ is virulently anti-Catholic). I loved the Catholic church from the first moment that I walked into it and I especially enjoyed Mass, which was then still in Latin and it had a grandeur to it that swept me away. I enjoyed fantasizing about the long tradition of the Catholic church, stretching back for centuries, back to the beginnings of Christianity. Its own authoritarian nature and self-proclamation of being the one true church was a convenient substitute for the now rejected authoritarianism of the Church of Christ, but I could make no move as long as I lived at home, or else I would not be living at home very long. I wasn't ready for that, not yet.

But soon I did break away. It was a wrenching process for it meant that, to a degree, I would be alienated from all of my family. Every member of both sides of my family was very devoted to the Church of Christ and, in their eyes, by my leaving it I was abandoning all hope of salvation. I was now the lone black sheep in the family and a genuine embarrassment to them all. Oddly, despite my years of religious indoctrination, I never considered that I could be wrong in my rejection of the Church of Christ.

When I went to college, Texas Tech University, which was then in its final few years as Texas Technological College, I started dating Linda, a Baptist. That year we attended both the First Baptist Church for her and the Catholic church for me, as well as a Missouri Synod Lutheran Church at times, just to see what it was like. At the end of the next summer, we married and started attending the Catholic church. Linda came to love it as much as I did and we began taking instruction. In the Spring of 1968, we both converted to the Catholic church. I had now found the new one true church.

Of course I didn't tell my family about my conversion. It was bad enough to have left the Church of Christ, but to become a Catholic was the worst form of apostasy and I couldn't imagine what kind of explosion there would be if they ever found out. When my dad died in December 1968, just as I was graduating, we were still unreconciled over religion and communication was just as difficult as ever.

However, my life as a Catholic was a short one. A few months after my conversion, during the summer of 1968, Pope Paul VI issued his encyclical *De Humana Vita*, condemning artificial means of birth control, to the shock of most Catholics I knew, as indeed it was to Linda and me. We thought his decision was wrong and we had no intention of following it. For many born Catholics, the encyclical apparently presented no problem -- they simply ignored it. But I was a convert with no intention of following the papal instruction, which led to my feeling like a hypocrite. My path was clear. I could no longer be a Catholic, but nothing else seemed appealing to me. I did give thought to Judaism, for it had an even longer tradition than Catholicism, but I soon discovered that trying to convert to Judaism was like trying to join someone else's family, for there was so much of a cultural component to it in addition to its religious aspects. I believed that I would always have remained an outsider.

As an undergraduate at Texas Tech I majored in History and especially loved the period of the Middle Ages. Upon graduation I went on to graduate school, earning a Master's degree in medieval history and continuing on in a Ph.D. program in East Asian history, all at Texas Tech University. After two years of doctoral work, I came to realize that attempting to have an academic career with all three of my degrees from the same university was not a wise move and if I were seriously interested in competing in the job market, I should leave Texas Tech for a larger university. Moreover, Linda and I had divorced and moving almost anywhere else seemed like a good thing to do.

After Linda and I divorced, I later married Pam and we moved to Jackson, Mississippi. She taught French at Tougaloo College, a predominantly-black college just outside of Jackson, and I worked in public relations and development there as well. We spent some time looking for a church there, but nothing seemed attractive, so we held our own religious services at home on Sunday mornings. We bought a biblical commentary and each Sunday I would read some verses from the Bible and then we would discuss their meaning, aided by the commentary. My old Church of Christ background came in handy, for I was very familiar with the Bible and by now I had been exposed to a great variety of theologies and biblical interpretations.

I was admitted to the Ph.D. program in medieval history at the University of Minnesota and Pam, our newborn son and I then moved to Minneapolis, her home town. We attended a Norwegian-language Lutheran church close to our apartment for about a year and when we moved to a different part of Minneapolis we went to a nearby Methodist church for a couple of years, and after that to a Presbyterian church. Pam was content with the Presbyterian church but Calvinism never appealed to me as it was too close to the outlook of the Church of Christ for me to embrace.

It was in Minneapolis that I developed asthma. When I went to the University of Minnesota student health service, I was told that they referred to asthma as "the PhD disease" because such disorders were so common among graduate students. At first I was still able to play sports and I was a member of the History Department intramural softball team. I held out the hope that once I completed my degree, my asthma would disappear.

After I received my PhD, we moved to Knoxville, Tennessee, where I taught at the University of Tennessee for a year. It was a very pleasurable experience and I loved both UT and Knoxville and I found very good friends in Paul and Mary Lee Bergeron. The dark spot was that my asthma worsened in Knoxville. It seems that every plant and spore in the world are to be found there and my lungs didn't react well to them. I began seeing a pulmonary specialist, and in a region known for Black Lung disease among coal miners, I was actually one of the healthiest patients in the waiting room.

We then moved to Oak Park, a suburb of Chicago, when I was appointed to a teaching position at the University of Illinois at Chicago Circle (now the University of Illinois at Chicago). However, by the time of our move to Chicago my marriage was nearly terminal. On Sundays Pam took our two children (my daughter had been born a few months after I graduated from the University of Minnesota) with her to a Presbyterian church while I stayed home and cleaned house. Two years after we moved to Chicago, we were divorced.

At the same time, my asthma continued to worsen. I had hoped that when I finished graduate school it would improve, then that when I got a tenure-track teaching position it would improve, then after Pam and I divorced that it would improve. Instead it steadily worsened. In 1981 I was hospitalized with an asthma attack for the first time, and during the period 1984-1987 I was in Intensive Care two to three times a year with serious asthma attacks, always life-threatening. I felt that I was becoming an invalid and whenever I left my apartment I would always do a pat-down to make sure I had my pocket inhaler of a bronchial dilator with me.

I was now completely jaded on organized religion in general, for the ten-year quest for the one true church had beaten me down and I had surrendered. I had considered very carefully the theology of each denomination that I had come across and tried to sift out what was true from what was untrue, but it had all become a blur as I could find no logical, rational reason to prefer one theology over another. To do so would be completely arbitrary, probably based on my own preferences, not the truth. My search to find God with my intellect had reached a dead end. In addition, I had been exposed to an entirely different way of looking at things spiritual. While in the doctoral program in East Asian history at Texas Tech, I had discovered Buddhism, to which I was instantly attracted, especially to Zen. Its non-logical, non-theological teachings affected me very deeply and reinforced my own experience of the hopelessness of attempting to determine the truthfulness of any denomination's teachings purely on a logical basis.

I simply abandoned the search and fell back on a basic image in Christianity, that of God as a father, the ideal father. If there was any truth in Christianity, then there must be truth in that image. I was now a parent and I was certain that if I knew that some serious harm would come to one of my children by an action of theirs, I would warn them personally. I would not leave cryptic messages in foreign languages lying around in the hope that they would find them and interpret them correctly. No, I would tell them myself directly and in plain language. I decided to rely on this premise. If I were about to inflict any serious harm on myself, God would have to let me know directly, for I would never get things sorted out in my mind by reading catechisms and creeds.

I was also left with a simmering dislike for organized religion. To me it was just so much man-made nonsense, a point that I would make frequently in conversations if given half a chance. For ten years I attended church only when I went to funerals or in order to please my grandfather when I would visit him back in Oklahoma. Religiously, I was nowhere and my spiritual life was barren. I had not had any religious experiences, no voices or visions. I had only thoughts about religion, not experiences, and I had never felt that I was in the presence of God. God seemed distant, remote and uncommunicative. Mysticism meant little to me and I didn't care for what little I knew little of it. In my university lectures I would brand Plato as a mystic and smirk when I related his belief that the only sure means of knowledge comes from divine revelation. One of the most famous mystics of the Middle Ages, my own period of study, is Julian of Norwich, and I though she was male. Well, just look at the name.

Later I would reflect that, with my illness, that is, what I had experienced in the Beyond, and my paralysis, I had been given the direct message that I had said I would wait for. Their wrenching effects on both my body and mind caused me to reflect on the adage, "Be careful what you ask for ..." while a Bible verse from my past came floating into my mind, which now seemed all too true, "it is a fearful thing to fall into the hands of the living God."

But as I came out of the coma at St. Bartholomew's, the memory of my experience and my self-judgment overwhelmed me. I was a failure. I was not the person that I had thought that I was. I was worthless. Thus at that one point early on in my confusing reentry into this life, I told my brother that he should just throw me in the trash, that I was worthless. He thought that I was giving up on life but he misunderstood completely, and yet he kept up his exhortations for me to suck it up and bear down. It was in my frustration that I tried to tell him bluntly what I thought of his exhortations.

The experience that I had in the Beyond was very different from what I would have thought that it would be like. The judgment on my life came from me, not from any other person, being or thing, and it was based not so much on deeds and actions as on the intention with which they were done. Doing what is right is very hard because it is very hard to know what is right. What is important is *wanting* to do what is right and sincerely trying to do so. The worth of our actions is based not on whether they are right or not but by what they say about who we are as people, what our motivations are.

There were some immediate lessons that I gained from my experience of the Beyond and review of my life. I felt differently about everything. As I later described my experience in my journal not long after being discharged from the hospital:

> *I FELT God for the first time that I could remember. I felt in the presence of God, and with God's help I could recover. I knew that I could not go back to my old ways. I also wanted other people's prayers to help me. I asked Keith to call Paul and Mary Lee (my very good friends) in Tennessee and ask them to pray for me.*

This was indeed a first, for never in my previous life would I have asked for help, especially for prayers.

The most transformative aspect of the entire experience was the life review in which I experienced others' experience of me, felt what they felt in our encounters. Now I am fully aware of the importance of treating all people with basic respect even when they are being obnoxious or provocative. No longer can I allow myself to respond with anger and harsh words when others are doing that to me.

This perspective is both liberating and frustrating in that it is extremely limiting. There are times when it would feel so good really to let someone have it, but I know that it is wrong. I have often thought that the world would be transformed if everyone had this same experience and really knew the concept of "do unto others" as a fundamental truth rather than as a pious adage. A few years after this experience I met the philosopher Robert F. Almeder, who wrote *Death and Personal Survival: The Evidence for Life after Death*, which explores a topic that naturally made him very interested in hearing about my own experience of the Beyond. After I recounted the life review, Bob said in a very serious voice, "Oh, I know some incidents in my life that I am not going to want to review." "Those are not going to be the ones that will shock you," I told him, "it will be the ones that you feel very confident about right now, that you are very OK with, that will completely humble you."

While I believe that when I was in the Beyond I was in the world of the divine, it was striking that it was a very non-denominational divine world. I came away with a strong sense of the purpose of life, of the unknowability of God, of what is OK and what is not, but there was no sense that any one system or viewpoint of God can possibly be exclusively right. I saw that there is truth in all of the various systems, but none of them are *the* truth. The truest picture of the various competing religious systems of the world is that of the Buddhist story of the blind men and the elephant. The different blind men felt a different part of the elephant, one the tusk, another the trunk, another the leg, another the tail, and so on. They then began describing the elephant, with one claiming that the elephant was like a snake, another that it was like a pillar, another that it was like a plow, and so on, and then they fell into vigorous argument, each one arguing that he was absolutely right and the others wrong. Of course each one was right for, based on his limited knowledge, he grasped a truth, but that limited knowledge was not *the* truth.

During my experience in the Beyond, I saw that time is a necessary fiction for this small perch in eternity that we occupy, but it is indeed a fiction. There are times when it seems that past, present and future are all one single and simultaneous continuum. *All that has or will happen has already happened, certainly I don't believe in the reality of time and I have had this feeling that everything has already happened, and I can't explain how that could be, it's just a feeling.* In later years this perception was strengthened by a number of confirming visions. *I was on the "el" and saw a young man, maybe about twenty-five. At the same time, I also saw him as an old man, sitting there, and at the same time he was also a baby as well. He was at that moment all that he was or ever will be, simultaneously. This particular image in itself meant nothing. He was being born and was already dead. He both existed and didn't exist. And so it is with all of us. At this moment, I am all that I ever was or ever will be. Time truly does not exist. I am not any one thing in particular. I can't be any one existence. For I have always been, yet I am only this at this moment.*

* * *

In my pain and frustration as I became adjusted to this bizarre new world that I was in, I would often feel that God was with me. I really did feel as though I would be able to move, and that the penetrating pain would help me move. As I prayed and tried to move something, again and again I heard a voice in my mind. It was my voice, but it wasn't *I* who was saying anything. It was just a voice. The words were always the same: "God in me." Just that. "God in me." I didn't really understand it, for I would have thought that something like "God with me," a version of the literal meaning of Emmanuel, "God with us," would have been normal or appropriate. But it was always the same, "God in me," and I was comforted.

Meanwhile, I had some very serious medical problems to deal with.

CHAPTER 3

Adjustment

Now fully conscious, I was aware of the succession of people coming by my bed, each person telling me warmly that I didn't know how lucky I was to be alive. After a few days I came to understand how true it was. The asthma which had been growing steadily more severe over the past years had this time very nearly killed me. My lungs had become so obstructed that I could not breath. I had been given the highest levels of all the medicines, just short of amounting to a toxic dose, and yet my lungs were not responding, so that they were keeping me alive by bagging me by hand in the Intensive Care Unit. They had given me everything they could that wouldn't kill me and yet my lungs were not working and I was barely hanging on to life.

In my passport I had listed my mother's name for next of kin to be notified in case of emergency. Certain that I was going to die, the hospital had notified my family that someone should come over England to pick up my body. My brother, who had never been to Europe or even out of the country, quickly got an emergency passport and airline ticket and arrived in London, expecting to be there for two or three days as he made the arrangements to have my body returned home. It turned out to be six weeks of crises for him to deal with.

When I returned to England in April of the following year, Dr. Hinds told me that the nursing strategy in the intensive care unit was based on the certainty that I would die. My condition warranted having a specific team assigned to me, but when the patient dies under such conditions it is very difficult emotionally on the medical team that has gotten so close to the patient. Thus it was decided that I would be treated like the other patients in the ICU and the normal rotating staff would attend to me.

However, one nurse, Sally Parr, objected to this strategy. As she later told me, she argued that my condition dictated that I should have a specific team caring for me. Discontent at the decision not to do this, she circumvented it by devoting all of her spare time to me. The rotation of the ICU staff explained the inconsistent accents that I had heard and constantly changing faces that I had seen. Through all of that confusion and pain, Sally was the one constant in my foggy first days out of the coma. Her face, framed by her lovely long, dark hair, radiated the care that she felt. This was the one good thing that I recognized in the entire confused jumble of my life there during those early days. I craved to see Sally more and was impatient when she wasn't there. The hope of seeing her helped get me through the worst of the confusion and pain of that first week of consciousness. However, at the end of that first week she left on holiday. On her last day at Barts she came to me and leaned over the bed, and looked at me squarely in the eyes.

"Steve," she said, "I am going on holiday now for several weeks, so you might be gone by the time I return. I want to you to be certain to write me after you get back to the States and let me know how you are doing." I nodded that I would, she turned and walked away and I never saw her again while I was in St. Bartholomew's. It was a terrible loss to me and for a while I felt abandoned and very alone.

About the time that Sally left, I came to understand that it was indeed true, I really should be dead. After my experience of the Beyond, I knew that I should have a tombstone that read "Failure." I didn't know what the future was going to be like, but I wanted another chance at life, so that the next time I died, the tombstone would not read "Failure," but "At Least He Tried." I wanted a chance to try harder to be the person I wanted to be. Thus I felt tremendous sadness and regret over my past life and at the same time I had unlimited optimism over the future. All would be well. However, I didn't trust myself. Too easily I gave up and I was very afraid that I would go back to my old life and my old ways of being that I now rejected.

One other thing happened, a truly bizarre event in my bizarre world. I also felt directed to go to the Episcopal Church -- the Anglican Church. I wish I could say that I felt that God had directed me, but it isn't true. I just felt absolutely certain that I should go to the Episcopal Church, by whom or by what I didn't know, but the message was unmistakable. The Episcopal Church? Why? I knew very little of it. I had attended its services one time, in Jackson, Mississippi, and had not liked it. I had attended it only one other time, when I was in Knoxville, Tennessee, visiting my friends Paul and

Mary Lee, although I usually did not go to church with them when I was there. But on the occasion that I did attend with them it was because I had been reading the works of Alan Watts and wanted to see if I could understand what he had written about the experience of a liturgical service, of being just one unit of a larger body. I was not overly impressed. This new direction was confusing. I hated institutional religion and had said so frequently over the previous ten years. I could not imagine why this was something I should do, but I was in no mood to question anything that seemed to come from whatever is beyond.

Altogether I spent four weeks in ICU, the first two weeks in a coma, and the third week is wrapped in fog with only a few shadowy memories remaining. My inability to speak was a problem. They had tried to work out a communication system by pointing to letters on a board, which I can remember only vaguely. However, that method was apparently too slow and for some reason didn't seem to work. They got a pad and some markers for me to write with, but my hands didn't seem to work, either.

They also tried some sort of microphone that was placed against my throat, trying to magnify the faint sounds that I was making. That, too, failed. Nothing helped until Dr. Hinds took that ring out of my throat. Then I could speak, but only with a very raspy voice. As it turned out, there was some paralysis in my vocal cords, a trace of which still remains in my often hoarse or raspy voice.

As soon as the cobwebs cleared from my head and this one reality persisted in the place of all the others, I no longer believed that the hospital staff had kidnaped me and paralyzed me. My brother didn't have a flying Kharmann Ghia. The de Boers twins from South Africa turned out to be the distinctively singular but very memorable Maura Falvey from Ireland. Those other bizarre worlds—the military hospital, the drug den, the scenes in Louisiana, and, sadly, the wonderfully warm house in the woods—must not have been true. However, apparently there had been some difficulty in shaving me, for indeed I did have a moustache growing now. Even though I now rejected those other possible realities as false ones, it is striking that the reality at St. Bartholomew's and all of the events that have followed in linear progression are no more real to me than those other possibilities that turned out to be ephemeral. Moreover, all of them, including this present world still feel far less real than did the Hyper-Reality of the Beyond, which possessed an intensity and unique reality that are indescribable. I have never been tempted to wonder if the Beyond were simply another hallucination, for it was far too intense and hyper-real. All of those other realities and this present world are, compared to the Beyond, analogous to a dream that we may have when we are sleeping compared to the apparent reality of this present world when we are awake.

It soon became clear to me that I had experienced hallucinations, dreams and visions, but there also were simple misunderstandings. Several years later I was talking with Hazel, the Welsh nurse in the ICU, laughing with her at my delusions and I mentioned the frightening hallucination of the African across from me, mauled by a lion, who had body parts removed by the nurses and stored in the cabinets under the windows. She took delight in telling me what really happened. The man was real and indeed was African, but he had suffered a heart attack, not an unfortunate encounter with an English lion. They had put foam rubber around him to keep him from moving around and at night they would come in and replace the foam rubber, stuffing the used padding into plastic bags and placing them in the cabinets under the windows. The foam rubber was light pink in color. In my confusion, paranoia and weak vision I had transformed the foam rubber into body parts removed from my roommate.

I did discover one contribution to my general confusion as I was coming back into consciousness. Majka, my friend from Sweden, told me that she was encouraged to talk to me while I was in the coma, for they assured her that I could hear her. I must have heard her, along with my brother and all the other people who were speaking to me. Somehow my brain tried to turn all of that disconnected information into a coherent picture or several coherent pictures. Since then I have advised people that indeed they should talk to people who are in a coma, but perhaps the number of people who speak to them should be limited and the content of the messages ought to be kept simple and uncomplicated.

My negative attitude towards the hospital staff largely lifted. I came to see them as truly wonderful and caring people. But I still was not in the best of spirits. My head still felt fuzzy and the pain in my feet and legs was still hideous. I felt like I was in a time warp, stuck in a single room, completely isolated from the rest of the world. The one exception to my more generous spirit was Dr. David Watson, an American. At first I had taken a deep dislike to him. During that very foggy third week, there had been talk of my repatriation back to Chicago. My memory is that he told me that there was a possibility that I might be able to be taken back home in three more days. "Not tomorrow," he said in what I took to be an extremely condescending tone, "not the day after that, but the day after that." He was talking to me as though I were a complete idiot and I resented it. I also disliked the hospital staff's standing around my bed discussing me in third-party terms as though I were not there or couldn't hear them or didn't have the wits to understand. I am a person, I kept thinking. I have feelings. I am not a he, I am me.

A few days later my opinion of Dr. Watson changed radically. I think that it was late at night, although I had no real sense of time sealed away from the world in my little room, and I was in my usual nighttime agony of pain, able to sleep only for short, fitful periods. Then Dr. Watson appeared out of the darkness of the dimly lit room. He asked me in the kindest voice, "How are you doing? I don't mean physically, I mean how are *you* feeling?"

In the more than half dozen times that I had been in ICUs in the previous four years with my chronic asthma attacks, never had a physician expressed an interest in the condition of my inner person. I remember letting it all out -- my confusion, my pain, my fears. Now that I was mostly lucid, it was such a relief to be able to express it all. I saw Dr. Watson as a genuinely kind man and soon I understood how truly confused I had been, what a difficult patient I had been, and I understood why he had spoken to me the way that he had. I spent much time apologizing to the staff for my behavior, which now embarrassed me. They all laughed it off, explaining that my confusion was typical of patients in my condition and they were used to it.

To my great disappointment, Sally never returned from her holiday. She had been my anchor during those difficult early days as I was coming back into consciousness and I missed her terribly. She had asked me to keep in touch, but I wondered if I would ever see her again. Majka, too, left, around the end of week four.

The hospital staff with whom I had contact were wonderful and I began to see each day as a gift, filled with wonder. My sadness at Sally's absence was relieved by getting to know the other nurses better. It was in this week that Maura Falvey (the erstwhile de Boers twin) and another nurse were in my room. "Steve," Maura asked me, "how would you like to stand up?" I was surprised, wondering how they would possibly arrange it, but, after being on my back for a month, any change would be good and I eagerly said yes. The two of them put my arms around their shoulders and raised me up, which of course, was much easier than it might have been because of my severely emaciated condition. As my body moved to the vertical, everything inside of me gurgled and shifted, which felt so very odd and made my head swim. I remember Maura looking up at me, my left arm around her shoulder, and saying, "My, you are tall, aren't you?"

Sometimes during that week they would put me upright in a large, red padded chair that stood to my left in the room, close to the door, with pillows stuffed around me to keep me in position, but it didn't work out very well. I couldn't keep my head upright for very long and soon it would slowly sag over to one side where it would remain until someone noticed and straightened it again. When I was in high school and worked at a pharmacy, I would make prescription deliveries to Old Folks' Homes. I had seen the residents there, sitting in their wheel chairs, with their heads slumped over to one side. I had pitied them before and now I was one of them. I wondered if I would ever regain control of my head.

There was another nurse there whose name, to my regret, I never learned or perhaps simply can't remember. She too was Irish, I think, and her hair was blondish. Like Sally, she would pay special attention to me, which I appreciated. There was a relatively quiet night in the ICU and she came to me and said "Steve, I would like to do something special for you." I was completely surprised, unable to imagine what she could mean although my mind raced with possibilities. "What?," I croaked out in my weak, reedy voice. "I want to wash your hair," she replied with the kindest tone. Oh what a gift! I was overwhelmed with gratitude. I didn't feel clean and I knew that my hair was a mess. Who knows when it had last been washed? I could feel my stiff hair when I moved my head on my pillow and I knew that it was dirty and sticky with some of the glue from the EEG still sticking in it.

That was a wonderful night, helping to take me away from the severe pain that was my constant companion during the night. It had to be a sponge bath and, because I was confined to my bed, it was not easy washing my hair. I was moved to the end of the bed, with my head extending out over the end of the mattress, and a bucket was placed under my head. Then wonderful, warm water was poured over my hair. It was exquisite, one of the most welcome, most sensuous things that I have ever felt. Then the shampoo was rubbed into a lather in my hair and more wonderful warm water was poured over my head. And then it was all repeated again, followed by an exquisite toweling of my hair. When it was over, I felt clean for the first time since had come back to consciousness and my self image soared. I thought she was the most wonderful person in the world. Every time I thought about her, I cried in appreciation for the humaneness with which she treated me.

I also came to like Andy Way, a male nurse. He seemed short (but of course my perspective was from a position flat on my back most of the time so it might not be an accurate one) but extremely muscular. He had a thick moustache, very bright blue eyes and an extremely outgoing and engaging personality. One evening, perhaps a week after my lovely hair washing, he asked me, "How would you like to have a real bath?" That, too, sounded wonderful. As delicious as my sponge bath and shampooing had been, after almost four weeks in the ICU, I must have needed a good soaking very badly. I heard the water running in a tub in room across the hall and then Andy came in and in one move scooped me up off the bed rather easily and carried me in to the tub. He set me down in the warm water so carefully. The water was wonderfully soothing but there was one problem -- my rear end seemed to be on top of a large, hard object. "Have you put me down on a rock?," I asked him. Andy let out a hearty laugh. "No, no," he said, "its your own tailbone, you've lost so much weight that you have nothing back there anymore." Despite my rear-end discomfort, soaking in a tubful of warm water was another indescribably wonderful experience.

Towards the end of that week, I was given actual food to eat. Up to then, the feeding tube had done the job (it was the feeding tube that had been tied around my right ear, causing so much pain to both ear and nose). Of course my useless hands and arms meant that I had to be fed. Andy asked me, "Would you like to feed yourself?" I looked at him as though he were crazy, not comprehending how it could be possible. Nevertheless, with some wariness I said that I would. Andy produced a large spoon and planted it in my right hand, between thumb and index finger, and then clamped his own thumb down securely over mine, pressing it down on the spoon. Holding both the spoon and my hand firmly, he dipped the spoon down into the stew and raised it up to my mouth. We ate and we repeated this process until the stew was gone. It was a delicious stew and a gratifying meal because I felt that, in a way, I had been helping myself and I didn't feel completely helpless. I was so very grateful to Andy for that one small act.

Andy also gave me my first excursion outside of my room. Majka was now back in Sweden and called me in the ICU. However, the phone was at the nurses' station in the main room. Andy came in, told me I had a call and said he would take me to the phone. He grabbed the bed and pushed it out the door, turned left down the short corridor, into the main ICU to the telephones. It was good to be able to talk to Majka now that my head was much clearer, but it was also marvelous to get outside of my room. I had been feeling very much like the cave dwellers in Plato's *Republic*, chained facing a wall while the shadows of passers-by danced against the cave wall. My entire world since regaining consciousness had been in the one room. There were windows to the outside world to my right but they were high on the wall and offered me no real view. There was door to my left, but its window was covered by blinds. When the door was open I could see another room on the opposite side of the hall, but nothing more. I could hear people passing by but I didn't know what lay beyond that door. Now my world had expanded considerably and I discovered that there really were other patients in that ICU.

I also took a strong liking to Jim Allen, another nurse. He seemed frail and thin, reminding me of Peter O'Toole. One night he stopped by my room before going on a shift in the Cardiac Care Unit. He was wearing a very military style uniform, a white tunic with stripes on the shoulder tabs. I laughed and asked him what he was wearing. Instantly I felt bad for laughing, for I didn't want to hurt his feelings. He was very kind and really talked to me with genuine conversations.

It was his kindness that really carried me through one of the roughest moments of that fourth week. Apparently during the second week in ICU I had been given something to combat the severe diarrhea that struck me along with the high fevor. The medicine had worked extremely well. I was asked if my bowels had been opened and, frankly, I wasnt sure what was meant. Did that phrase simply refer to a bowel movement, or did it mean had something been done to break the log jam, that is, had I been given some medicine to get my bowels working again? Now they gave me something to restore proper functioning to my bowels although, in my paralyzed condition with my inability to take care of myself and thinking only in the short term, I was just as happy that my bowels had been quiet.

At first nothing happened, so I was given some additional medicine. Jim assured me that I need not worry, for it wasn't very strong. Then things started moving. I told Jim that I might need a bedpan and he brought something called the little pan. He slipped it under me but it was cold and very shallow and it really hurt my bony back end. Then the medicine really began kicking in and I felt as though my intestines were being ripped out of their moorings. On the positive side, however, the pain was so intense that it completely took my mind off the pain in my feet. At last my bowels began moving and continued to do so for what seemed like an eternity. I thought the agony would never stop. The pain was so dreadful and yet, at the same time, it was indeed the greatest relief that I had ever felt. It seemed to go on and on.

At last it was over. I was completely drained of energy and awash in my own sweat. Jim came over and comforted me, "What a good job you've done," and he added, "Your mother would be proud of you." He told me not to worry about the mess and he and Hazel cleaned everything up. I sank back on the bed panting and totally exhausted.

My brother Keith also made a few appearances during this week, but it seemed that he wasn't there very often, for somehow he had found a girlfriend. I couldn't imagine how he was able to have done this in such a short time, but there was an Australian woman who had a relative also in the ICU at St. Bartholomew's. Keith brought her to my room once to introduce me to her, but my mind was still groggy and I don't remember much about her, except that she was very attractive. Keith later told me that her name was Amanda Muggleton and she was a singer and actress in Australia. One movie of hers in particular that he mentioned to me, because of the country and western music in it, was *Queen of the Road*. Understandably Keith had found it far more pleasant to spend time with her than to while away the hours at St. Bartholomew's.

I did have time to reflect during this week as well. The paralysis seemed like such an appropriate problem for me to have. I had certainly been stuck emotionally, seemingly unable to get on with my life and fixated on the problems that I had been having with the woman I had dated for three years, up until just before my illness in London. But more than that, I had always been proud of my independence. I didn't mind helping other people, but I hated for people to help me, for I didn't want to put them to any trouble on my account. And now, here I was, virtually helpless, dependent on others for my every need. What a hard way to learn an important lesson. I saw that some people actually seem to like helping me, and my helplessness and neediness were allowing them to show care, compassion and love. My previous pride and stubbornness had deprived others of an opportunity to express those feelings. Instead of not being a problem for them, I had been a pain. That was over now for I was deeply grateful for every act of kindness that came my way. The world was filled with kind people and I had never noticed before.

CHAPTER 4

Miracles

At the beginning of week five, because I was no longer critically ill, I was moved out of the ICU and transferred to Radcliffe Ward, a unit for patients with neurological problems. I was very nervous and apprehensive about being moved and forced to give up the only home I had known at Barts and by now I was now very attached to the ICU staff. My new room was a large one, with four beds, two on each side of the room. Mine was closest to the windows on the left side. I could see out of the windows a bit, which was something new, and I could even feel the warm summer breeze blowing across me. I marveled at how such a simple sensation could be so pleasant. At times I could catch the scent of car exhaust and diesel, and it seemed as though the air were alive. A row of windows ran along the wall between the room and the hallway, allowing me to see people passing by. I had three ward mates, so this was a much less isolated existence and it was good, but I missed everyone in ICU. I felt especially alone.

Because I was paralyzed, I required constant nursing attention, which was ordered by the hospital, and I had my own private nurses around the clock in eight-hour shifts.

There was a constant rotation of private nurses ministering to my needs. Most were good, some wonderful, while a few needed to find a different way to make a living.

I believe that I was moved on July 10, a Sunday. My memory is that it was on the next day, Monday, that something happened that changed my physical condition. My nurse for that eight-hour shift was feeding me breakfast and it was very obvious that this was an unwelcome task for her. Her clearly signalled attitude was one of impatience, of putting up with something decidedly unpleasant, which really annoyed me. Dependence was something that had always been extremely distasteful to me and here I was dependent on others for everything. Her attitude hurt me and I felt both angry and determined.

Actually I did have some movement below my neck, for I could make my left shoulder move upwards, that is, I could give it a short shrug. After that unpleasant breakfast, for some reason I made a vow—by either Friday or Saturday of that week, I was going to feed myself. Of course I told no one of my resolution. I don't know why the vow was for Friday or Saturday, but that is what came into my mind. It seemed like a crazy ambition, for I had been told that the paralysis was likely to be permanent and now was I going to go from a slight shrug of the shoulder to feeding myself in four or five days' time? Nonetheless, I now began pouring all of my concentration into my left shoulder, trying to expand the movement to increase the lift. I was trying to harness all of my body's energy and send it into my left shoulder and make it move just a little bit more.

Then the miracles began. I could feel an energy flowing from outside of me, clearly something external pouring into my body. What is more, in my mind's eye, I could *see* that force. It looked like what I would expect electricity to look like, golden energy flowing through me. Moreover, inside my body, I could *feel* it, for it gave a slight buzzing sensation. I knew it was not my own energy and I knew I was not imagining it as in a visualization exercise. My mind was perfectly clear now. To me, it was divine energy. I kept remembering those comforting words that I had heard, "God in me."

My thought was that I did not know if this energy would heal me, but I felt certain that if I did not cooperate with it, I would not be healed. This was a chance, but only a chance, not a certainty. As a quadriplegic, I actually had very little else to do with my time and for four days I put all my concentration into connecting with that divine energy and attempting to channel it into my left arm and shoulder. I began to lift my shoulder higher and higher, and then I could move the arm slightly. I then concentrated, focusing that energy on that little bit of movement and expanding it by small degrees.

Slowly, the movement grew. From my prone position, I summoned all my strength and held my left arm straight up in the air. But not for long. After a second or two, the strength was spent, my arm bent at the elbow and my arm fell, with my left hand falling on my face, giving myself a sharp, stinging blow to the nose. I rested a bit, got in contact with that divine energy again, and again held my arm straight up. After a slightly longer delay, the strength was drained and I gave myself another blow to the nose. Over and over I went through this little ritual, although eventually I learned the basic maneuver of turning my head to the side when my arm collapsed, and with each effort I could hold the arm up in the air just a little longer than the previous time. After a couple of days, I could bend my arm at the elbow and pull the hand toward me. I practiced this little movement over and over again as my arm and hand moved in a very erratic and tortured motion, but I eventually could pull my left hand up to my face with a degree of control.

By Friday morning I felt ready. When my breakfast was brought, the nurse (a different one, for my nurses changed constantly) prepared to feed me. But I said, "I'll feed myself today." The nurse gave me an incredulous look. In a tone of complete unbelief, she said, "OK, give it a try."

The plate of toast was on a tray in front of me. I asked the nurse to move the tray so that it was almost up to my chin and I asked that the napkin be spread out under my chin. I reached out my left arm, threw my hand out so that it landed behind the toast and brought it forward, thus shoveling the toast into my mouth. It was not pretty, but it worked. Now the nurse had an even more unbelieving look on her face. I had triumphed. I had fed myself. From that meal on, I insisted on feeding myself at every meal no matter what was on the menu, even when it was stew, which is not really designed to be finger food.

In the first few days, it was extremely awkward, but my arm was getting better and better and I gained some ability to manipulate my fingers. No matter what the food was, I fed myself. I still could not grasp or hold a spoon or a fork, so I continued to scoop the food into my mouth. I would pick up what pieces I could and shove them into my mouth. When there was soup, it would be put into a cup with a lid to prevent severe spillage. Even though the strength in my left hand was increasing, I was still extremely weak. Once, in the middle of the following week, soup was the course and the nurse, a man of Indian background who was a medical student, poured it into the cup and he handed it to me. However, he did not wait for me to get a good grip on it but released it too soon. The cup slipped out of my feeble grip and the soup spilled on the bed. He was very apologetic, saying, "You look so strong now that I forgot how weak you really are."

Once I had triumphed in my self-feeding, I turned my attention to cooperating with the divine energy in the rest of my body. Again, I could see so clearly the golden, electrical energy flowing into me from beyond. I fixed my mind on connecting with it and helping conduct it through my arms and legs. Again and again I heard the voice say, "God in me."

By early in the next week, my sixth week at St. Bartholomew's, I gained some slight movement in my right arm and hand. Standing beside my bed on the right side was a very large tank of oxygen. The Thatcher cutbacks in the National Health Service meant that there could not be a constant supply of oxygen at every bed, so they had to use the oxygen tanks in wheeled stands that could be moved wherever they were needed. My lungs were still very fragile and the oxygen was always stationed there as a precaution. I was able to get my right hand up to one of the metal brackets of the stand and grasp it. I then pulled against the weight of the tank and its stand in an improvised isometric exercise. Steadily I gained a small degree of control over the movements of that arm.

I began to grow alarmed at my hands, for they had

suffered some serious muscle atrophy in them. There were areas on the back of each hand, under knuckles, that were sunken in, but worse than that, the lack of movement in my hands for five weeks was drawing my hands up into something resembling claws. Again I thought back to the prescription deliveries that I had made to the nursing homes when I was in high school, seeing the residents sitting in the wheel chairs, their heads slumped over to one side and their hands drawn up together into useless claws in their laps. And now, that was me. What to do?

I remembered back to my youth when I had to rebuild the strength in my hands and arms when I had broken an arm (which had happened three times, so I knew the routine very well). I asked Keith to buy me a couple of rubber balls, large enough to fit into my hands. He got them for me and I kept one in each hand almost all the time, squeezing them with my pathetic little grip for all I was worth. I even slept with them in my hands, hoping that this would prevent the claws from drawing up even more tightly.

Although I could move my left arm and hand, they were so weak that they were of limited use. That was made obvious when I had to deal with books, which I was eager to read simply for the change. A cart of books was brought up from the hospital library and I picked two. One was on Queen Victoria's children and the other on King Charles II's "Protestant whore," Nell Gwen. The first one was in large type, which was helpful because my eyes were still so bad. I could not see sharply for more than a few feet beyond me, with everything in the distance simply a blur. I asked Dr. Watson what was wrong with my eyes and he told me that

I had lost so much fluid from my body that my eyeballs had shrunk. Great, another problem. Would it improve or was I going to be virtually blind from now on?

I enjoyed reading, even though it was a bit of a struggle because of my poor vision. However, I was still very weak in general. I tired easily and often fell asleep while reading. Seeing me in that state, the helpful nurses would come by and place my book on the stand to the left of the bed, where it was lost to me. It might as well have been in the next room. Even though after Friday of week five I could flail my arm and sometimes reach the book with my hand, I had no strength in my hand and I could rarely pick up the book or hold on the book once I had it in my hand.

My poor hand control also caused a misadventure with chocolate. A tube of Cadbury's pieces was on the bedside table, looking very delicious and much lighter than a book. No assistance was nearby so I reached over and grabbed the tube and tried to pour some of the pieces into my mouth. But the tremble in my hand got the better of me and all I did was to dump out all the contents on my face and chest and the bed as well.

At first I was unhappy about being in Radcliffe Ward, with its four beds. When I had been in the ICU, I had been in a room with only one other patient. When I first arrived at my new quarters, I was quite shy but soon I came to like my three roommates. They were all friendly people and I enjoyed the visits paid them by their families. In general, there was so much more going on in this ward than in the isolation of my quarters in the ICU. My memory is not sharp for all of my wardmates, but I remember best the man who was in the bed next to mine, to my right. He had a brain tumor and was not doing well at all, which was all the sadder because he had a very young daughter. We enjoyed comparing our dislike for neurologists and their damned tests. "Smile," they would say to us, inspecting our faces for a lopsided grin. They would hold out their index and middle fingers spread apart and order us, "Squeeze them." "Squeeze them," they would repeat with more intensity, even though we were trying to do just that with all our might. We were supposed to hold an arm out and resist their efforts to push them down. My arm would collapse at the first pressure. We agreed on our least favorite test, the key dragged across the soles of our feet, a very painful and annoying procedure which we both hated. (A few years later I talked with a friend who had suffered a brain tumor, and she said that it was this very test that provided the clenching clue of her condition.)

There was also an effort dedicated to putting weight on my ravaged body. The illness and the paralysis had led to tremendous weight loss and muscle atrophy, leaving me with a badly emaciated body. Without more muscle mass my recovery would be even more difficult. St. Bartholomew's was one of the last hospitals in Britain that had not yet adopted the system of individual meals brought in to the patients on trays. At Barts, a large cart was rolled in to our room with all the entrées in large containers and our food was ladled out on our trays.

I had never been a lover of vegetables but now I found that I craved them, even the dreaded brussels sprouts, for now, amazingly, I found them to be utterly delicious. I came to believe that English hospital food was the height of fine dining. Moreover, I could have as much of whatever food

I wanted, including multiple desserts. In addition, special dietary supplements were prepared for me, designed to add calories and protein to my diet.

On the Sunday night of my second week in Radcliffe Ward I met Sophie. She came on as part of the rotation of my special nurses and instantly I took a strong liking to her. She came into the ward in her nurse's uniform, with her long, dark hair done up in a bun. Her large eyes and open, exuberant face seemed to embrace life to the fullest. Compassion, life and energy radiated from her face and, moreover, she was extremely thoughtful. When she discovered that I was an American, she brought me iced water (she had learned of Americans' love of this true delicacy from her American acquaintances at the University of Bath). In the mornings she was careful always to bring me my toast while it was still warm. I liked her a great deal and wanted to look my best for her. It was because of her that I decided that my moustache needed to go. Risking serious injury to my face, I took a razor in my left hand, constantly shaking with a pronounced tremble, and shaved it off. We instantly hit it off nicely and she asked to be able to stay working with me while I added in my own request for her to stay on. I was so grateful that it was agreed to and she stayed with me on the night shift for the remainder of my stay at Barts. Her shift was in the evening, starting about 8 p.m., and each day as that hour approached, I would eagerly stare out the windows to the hallway so that I could catch the first glimpse of her as she arrived. I was having great difficulty sleeping because of the pain in my feet and legs and our routine was that she would come and sit beside me after the final rounds of medicine were brought around about 10.30 or 11.00 at night. We would talk quietly in the dim light of the ward until it got much later and my pain pills and sleeping pills finally began to take effect. I would doze off and then awaken about dawn and see Sophie again. She would bring my warm toast before anyone else in the ward was awake and I would then begin my morning clean-up -- washing myself, trying to shave myself and brush my teeth as best I could given the difficulty that I had in holding a toothbrush. Then she would leave about 8 a.m. and I would count the twelve hours until she would arrive again. Much like Sally had been, Sophie was the continuity in my life.

There was a rather large black spot, however. Keith began to be a problem for me. He had been fine for most of the first days that I could remember, for he was enjoying being with Amanda. But then she had to return to Australia and Keith found himself without a diversion. For most of weeks five and six he was sullen and morose, complaining constantly about almost everything. His major complaint was that his hotel was too noisy and he couldn't sleep. (He had always had trouble sleeping for he really needed to sleep in a cave. At home he had put aluminum foil over his bedroom windows so that not a photon of light could disrupt his sleep.) He made it into my room in the late morning of each day and would simply sit there and mope. To his credit was the fact that he thought he would come to London and bring my corpse home in a few days. Those few days had now turned into a month and more and he was genuinely restless and unhappy.

Nonetheless, I didn't like the way he treated me.

My helplessness had made me even more sensitive to being treated as though I were an object instead of a real person with real feelings. Majka knew how much I like Kit Kats and when she left she saw to it that I had a nice supply of them. Keith would sit down in a chair by the bed and help himself to my stocks without asking. Once he did it right in front of me. "Go ahead and help yourself," I said, half sarcastically. "I intend to," he shot back, with a dark, determined look on his face. And what was worse, he would also swill my special iced water that Sophie made for me, again without asking. At other times he would sit in a chair close to the bed, with his legs crossed, and swing the top leg so that it kicked the bed. Over and over and over he would kick the bed. I wanted to scream at him. But I was so totally dependent on him that I felt it was best to watch what I said. I endured it as my resentment against him grew.

Meanwhile, my physical recovery continued. By Wednesday of the second week on Radcliffe Ward, I could move my left arm fairly well, and while I could move my right arm I couldn't lift it off the bed. I did my best to use my arms and help the nurses. When I would be bathed or when the sheets were changed, I tried to reach over with my left arm and grab the frame of the oxygen tank stand on my right and roll myself over on my right side to make it easier. There were some less than brilliant efforts. When I had bowel movements, I wanted to do as much for myself as possible and I tried to wipe myself. It was a dismal failure and all I did was smear everything around all over myself. It was an additional humiliation that I simply had to accept. And, I thought, this might be the rest of my life.

I could now move my right leg just a bit but not lift it

off the bed, and my left leg was still completely motionless. In discussing this with Pam Barber, the physiotherapist (or physio-terrorist as I found out they were sometimes called in Britain), she pointed out to me that legs make up a great percentage of one's body weight, and they are actually very heavy. Pam was fantastic. During week five, she would come to my room and move my arms and legs around in a range of motions. She said that even though I could not move them for myself, it would help reestablish the nerve connections simply if they were moved.

Wednesday night of week six, July 20, was a terrible one for pain. My legs and feet ached beyond belief and even my mental efforts to love the pain were not very effective. I was in agony. I slept fitfully and kept trying to direct the divine energy into my legs and feet, especially my right foot. I seemed to be able to feel my entire nervous system, to feel all of my nerves. The night seemed endless, with neither beginning nor end as I drifted in and out of troubled sleep. All I seemed to be able to feel was my right foot. Towards dawn I dozed off more soundly than usual. I awoke perhaps thirty or forty minutes later feeling slightly disoriented and totally tired out as I began my morning cleanup routine. However now my foot and legs felt different to me. I looked down at them and an impulse struck me. I raised them both off the bed, even the left one, which less than an hour before I could not move at all! I was amazed. I could even bend both of them at the knee and I could flex my right foot up and down. In addition, I could raise up my right arm. I was in utter astonishment. This was incredible. Now I could move everything except for my left foot.

When the morning routine started at the hospital, the nurses usually came and put up an incline at the head of my bed so I could sit up, and then they would scoot me up onto the incline. But this morning, after they lowered the incline, I told the nurse, "I can do it myself". She stood back, looking skeptical. To her amazement (and even to mine, frankly), all on my own I pulled my heels back up against my butt, dug my heels in, and gave a shove, scooting myself up against the incline. Both of us were astonished. Perhaps an hour later, I heard someone coming down the hall at a very fast pace. It was the neurologist, who only two weeks earlier had told me that the paralysis would probably be permanent. His face showed utter shock. He had been told of what I had done and now asked me to do it again. I did. Once again I pulled my heels up to my butt, dug them in, and kicked myself upright. He was stunned. He stroked his chin and started talking to me in a slow, deliberate voice, saying that he had never seen anything like this. "Sometimes we are inclined to be rather gloomy in our prognosis," he said, adding that he had no explanation for how I was able to do what I had just done. I knew of one, but it wasn't scientific so I kept it to myself.

I was eager to show off my new abilities to Sophie, but I had to wait all day long before her shift started. At last evening came and I recognized the pace of her steps advancing down the hallway. I looked out the windows to the hallway for her, and finally she appeared. I raised my right arm, which just the night before I had been unable to lift, and gave her a weak wave, more of a fluttering of my hand than a proper side-to-side wave. Sophie smiled and waved back. Then she did a second take, came to a complete stop and stared at me. I waved again. With the brightest, warmest smile she came rushing into the room, full of questions—how had I done that, when did it happen, what had happened?

So now almost everything moved. All that was still paralyzed, at least that I knew about, was my left foot. I could not move it up or down, a movement called the dorsal flex. I was anxious to get home. I had been having dreams of being in a rehabilitation unit in Chicago, of splashing around in a water tank. By no means was I being neglected at Barts, but I really needed intensive therapy and imagined that back home would be the best place for that, which was also the opinion of the physicians at St. Bartholomew's.

In week six, I was taken to the therapy room. This was a big event. For the first time in five weeks, I was going into the outside world. They had to lift me into the wheelchair, which was easier than it might have been due to my massive weight loss. I would then be covered with a blanket and taken down the elevators, outside and into a different building. This was exciting and yet at the same time I was fearful. I couldn't see very well so most of the outside world was nothing but a blur. At the same time, it scared me. I was helpless, unable to fend for myself, unable even to wheel myself along. It was a frightening world in which I did not feel that I belonged. At times people in the hospital hallways and elevators or on the outside would stare at me as I was being pushed along in the wheelchair. However, the trip into the outside world was rich in sensations. It was filled with new sights and colors, new sounds and especially new smells. Even the heavy odor of motor exhausts was still a thrill.

Unfortunately I could do nothing to assist them in moving me on and off my bed, or in and out of the wheelchair. I couldn't control my legs and my arms were too weak to bear any weight. One day there was no orderly to lift me into the wheelchair and one of the sisters on Radcliffe Ward, Sister Jessie Wong from Borneo, took command. Even though she was a very small woman, she positioned herself just so and threw me over her shoulder and deposited me easily in the wheelchair. And when I had finished the therapy and was returned to the room, again she found the right position and hoisted me out of the chair, over her shoulder again and back onto the bed. While I no longer weighed all that much, if I could have stood up, I would have been a foot taller than she. "How did you do that?," I asked her in amazement. "Mind over matter," she stated with assurance.

The therapy was basic—more movements of my arms and legs. But also I was strapped on a tilting table and they began the process of getting me reacquainted with being upright. It felt so very odd to have gravity pulling at my insides. Again, as when Maura had helped me into an upright position over her shoulders two weeks earlier, everything inside of me gurgled and shifted and I felt slightly nauseous. But the tilting table brought a new surprise. As I began to reach the upright position, I felt a sharp sticking sensation in my left thigh. "I think someone has left a pin in my pajamas," I told them. They searched but found nothing. Yet every time I was raised up, I felt the pin jabbing into my thigh. This was a painful mystery.

During that sixth week, as I slowly regained strength, I was given a new exercise to do. I was to sit on the edge of the bed and attempt to hold my torso upright. Because all my muscles everywhere had been destroyed, including those in my chest and abdomen, this simple exercise was extremely difficult. My body wanted simply to slump over forward, with my chin against my chest. It hurt to try to pull the great weight of my torso upright and I could do it for only a few seconds before the muscles broke and I slumped down again. I could foresee that there was going to be a lot of rehabilitation ahead. In my emaciated state, the frequent slumps forced my ribs into my abdomen, which soon became sore to the touch. As I was preparing to return to Chicago, Pam, the physiotherapist, wrote a letter to whomever my physical therapist there would be. As she handed me the letter she said, "Steve, this has been a very difficult assessment to write, for your condition changes so much from one day to another."

During the last few days of mys tay at St. Bartholomew's, the staff began to be concerned about some of the side effects of my paralysis. After all, I was now in the sixth week of non-movement. One of the mechanisms by which blood is returned from the legs back up to the heart is the squeezing of the leg muscles when one walks, so blood can pool down in the legs of those who are bedridden, which can then lead to blood clots in the legs. They brought some long anti-thrombosis stockings, teddy stockings they were called, for me to wear. Unfortunately, the only ones that they had were too small, but they would have to do. Because they were too small they were also tighter than they were supposed to be and thus it was very difficult to pull over my legs even as thin as they were. They looked a bit ridiculous, I thought, but I kept telling myself that they were necessary.

Another problem for those who don't walk for a long period of time is foot drop. With the lack of stretching that normally comes with walking, the achilles tendons contract, making it impossible to lift the feet properly, which results in the feet sort of dangling at the end of the leg. A board was brought to fit across the foot of my bed. The soles of my feet rested firmly against the board, thus lifting my foot up and stretching out the tendon. I was grateful for the effort to control the problem, but I also began to see that even if I regained full use of my legs and even could walk again, I could have permanent problems in just getting around.

In preparation for my return home, I needed my own pajamas. I asked Keith to buy them for me. He asked me what kind I wanted. "I don't really care very much," I answered, " but I certainly don't want anything pink." He came back with pink pajamas that were much too big for my emaciated body. The phrase "passive aggression" began to sneak into my mind. When I finally did put them on, the material around the waist had to be drawn together and held with a big safety pin.

The biggest obstacle to my return to Chicago were my lungs, for they had to be functioning well enough that the long flight home would not be a risk for me. I began to focus the divine energy to clear up my lungs, picturing that golden divine light flowing into my lungs. My lungs did respond, steadily improving during the two weeks on Radcliffe Ward, but of course I was still on high levels of medicine to help keep my lungs open. The objective was to stabilize my condition in preparation for my return home. My big test was set for Thursday of week six. If I could pass the pulmonary test, I could be released for my repatriation, the technical term for going home.

And then disaster struck. On the very day of the test, an overly officious *locum tenens*—a physician brought in on a temporary basis in order to allow the regular staff some time off—suddenly showed up in the ward. He took a look at my chart and decided that my treatment was all wrong and ordered a complete change in my medicine. His actions were not actually wrong, for they might have been proper for a normal patient. Had he bothered acquainting himself with my medical history he would have known that that I was the prize patient and we were trying to get my situation stabilized so that I could return home. He then decided to give me his own pulmonary test. He brought out a peak-flow meter (which one blows into, indicating how much air one can move out of the lungs) and told me to exhale into it. I refused, because several years earlier after one of my especially severe hospitalizations for asthma, I had a comprehensive pulmonary examination and it was discovered that my lungs spasm very easily and that my lung function falls off markedly after a peak-flow test. At that time I was counseled never to take that test. But the *locum* was not taking no for an answer. After a couple of my refusals, he jammed the meter into my mouth, held my nose and forced me to exhale. I began to panic and my breathing deteriorated badly. I was now wheezing very loudly.

My brother hurriedly set out in search of Dr. Watson, who soon showed up and took charge of the situation. He put an end to my unplanned pulmonary test and countermanded the change in my medication. He explained that the changes weren't necessarily wrong, but rather inappropriate for my overall condition and for our objective.

As I was resting, trying to recover my calm and get control of the wheezing, a fellow I had never seen before showed up at my bed. "Professor Fanning?," he asked. I knew something important had happened, for up to that moment everyone had been addressing me as Steve or Steven. He introduced himself as the hospital manager. He gave his deep apologies for what had happened to me. He said that it was not the first time in which that *locum* had been out of line and he added that the physician had now been released from his employment at St. Bartholomew's. Not feeling very Zen-like after my morning ordeal, I considered that to be very welcome news which I greeted with joy.

But meanwhile, I had about two hours left before my crucial pulmonary test and I was wheezing noisily. I was bathed in sweat from the sudden trauma and from my own anxiety. I renewed my concentration technique in earnest, attempting to calm my lungs and get them back to the state they were in before my unplanned examination. It was around 2 p.m. when the pulmonary specialist showed up with his digital meters. Being as calm as I could be under the circumstances, I did my best to blow into the meter, expelling as much air as I could with great force, to demonstrate that I was doing well enough to return home. When the tests were over and I was trying to regain my breath after the huffing and puffing, he attempted to print out the results. To my utter horror he discovered that the battery in his machine was dead. There were no data. The tests would have to be repeated.

I couldn't believe this but I had no choice but do it over if I wanted to go home. Quickly I returned to my visualizations. After a fresh battery was inserted in the meter, I went through the tests a second time. Now there were data. I worked at catching my breath as the strip of paper containing the results was expelled from the machine. The numbers were excellent, far better than anyone could have hoped for. I was going to go home!

In fact, the results were too good. The chief pulmonary specialist was summoned to examine the data. He didn't believe that my lungs could have performed that well, thus he didn't trust the accuracy of the figures. He wanted to repeat the test to make sure the results were valid. Not again, not a third time (really, a fourth time if the unplanned tests of the *locum* are counted)! Once again, I had no choice if I wanted to go home any time soon. Again I expelled air for all I was worth and again the results were excellent. He cleared me for repatriation.

However, the next problem was insurance. My HMO was balking at paying for the repatriation. They were insisting that I should just stay at St. Bartholomew's until I could return home on my own two legs. But of course no one could say when that might be. It could be next week or in two years or never. I was angry and frustrated, for I needed intensive physical therapy that was not available at the hospital and in this the physicians at St. Bartholomew's heartily agreed. I needed to come home immediately. Keith had been handling the situation, talking with the HMO, with the physicians, and with my mother and Tullie, my stepfather. After I had passed the pulmonary test and was

Above, enjoying life in Sweden, 1988.

Left, 60 lbs lighter after the London experience.

cleared to go home, the HMO gave their final denial. They would not pay for my repatriation. Now what?

Dr. Hinds knew that TWA would arrange the repatriation for about $16,000. But Keith had met a Canadian woman at the hospital whose husband had suffered either a stroke or a heart attack while on a cruise in the Soviet Union, and they were arranging his repatriation to Vancouver. That company, Europe Assist, would arrange everything for $10,000. Even if it were a bargain, I did not have that kind of money and I was stuck.

But then Keith told me that Tullie had said that if the HMO would not pay for my repatriation, he would do it, generosity for which I was extremely grateful. But in the meantime, the money had to be paid now. This was far beyond the credit limit on my normal credit card, so Keith took my American Express card and used it. I could not worry at this moment about what to do once the bill arrived. I could fret about that later, at my leisure.

I would be leaving the next day, Friday of week six. It was almost too soon. I didn't know how I could leave Sophie, for I had grown deeply attached to her and she was now an essential part of my life. It had only been since Monday that we had gotten to know each other but she had become my lifeline, my connection with someone outside of myself. I was hopelessly in love with her and I knew that she returned at least some of my feelings. I talked with Sophie about my departure the next day. I could confide to her about my hopes and my fears.

I really did need to get home, for I knew that affairs there had to be a mess. My two-week vacation had turned into an eight-week absence, with my being almost completely out of communication. (Actually at some point in week four, my brother brought me some get-well cards and letters that had arrived in London, but I couldn't really hold them in my hands, my eyes had trouble focusing on them, and my memory was so bad that I didn't recognize who had sent them anyway.) My rent hadn't been paid, my bills hadn't been paid, child support hadn't been sent in (the state frowned on such negligence, and while I didn't consider myself a dead-beat dad, technically now I was one). I had been scheduled to teach a summer session course at the university and I wondered what had happened with it. I didn't even want to think about what awaited me, but I knew it had to be taken care of soon or matters would be much worse. Terms like eviction and law suits were clawing at the back of my mind, adding to my anxiety about how I would manage my physical condition upon my return. I began to wonder if I could even write checks so that I could pay my bills. I got a pencil and some paper and with my newly useable right arm and hand tried to sign my name. My hand trembled rhythmically as I held the pencil and tried to write. I pondered the unfamiliar signature. It had no resemblance to my signature that was on file at my bank but it did make me think of my grandfather's writing about the time he died of Alzheimer's at age ninety. This was still another sign that I had such a long way to go to recovery.

I didn't doubt that soon I would be able to stand up and to walk, but how long would it take? I told Sophie that my ambition was to walk within two weeks of my return home. Wisely she cautioned me, "You really must to take things easily and not set unrealistic expectations for yourself." I confided all my worries to her, for it was hopeless to try to talk with my brother and I unloaded my fears to the ever patient Sophie. Even though I could move my legs, they were incredibly weak and I still couldn't flex my left foot. How would I be able to push down the clutch and actually drive my car when I got home? Would I be confined to my apartment? I lived alone, so how would my basic needs be met? Sophie listened to me and encouraged me. I did not want the night to end nor did I want to sleep away any of the last remaining time that I had with Sophie.

On this last night in St. Bartholomew's, Dr. Watson dropped by, just to talk and to say goodbye. He must have stayed with me for an hour. He told me how happy he was at my rapid recovery and I let him know how grateful I was to everyone at the hospital. He mentioned that there was talk of closing down St. Bartholomew's in an economy move by the National Health Service. He then began an eloquent elegy to Barts. It had been founded in the 1120s by a charter from King Henry I and it was here that Harvey discovered the circulation of the blood. After discussing the important role that St. Bartholomew's had played in medical history, he suddenly changed his point. "Barts is not a place", he said, "it is not a collection of buildings. It is people, it is us, all of us here, working to help the patients that come to us." And I am one of those lucky patients, I thought.

Sophie and I talked late into the night, neither of us wanting the night to end. I asked if she would do something for me, would she give me a kiss. She did, and it was exquisite. In time I did doze off despite my being pulled between excitement and dread. Morning came. My fears were rampant and my heart was pounding. I needed to get home but, oddly, St. Bartholomews also felt like my home for it was here that I had entered my second life. Here I was taken care of and I was safe. How could I leave this? How could I give up Sophie, probably never to see her again? What would actually happen to me once I got back to Chicago? Would I ever recover enough to resume my normal life? I had only questions awaiting answers. I knew that somehow everything would be alright, but there might be a lot of difficult times to reach that point.

It was the morning of July 22, 1988. As I was moved from Radcliffe Ward and rolled down the corridors of St. Bartholomew's to the ambulance waiting to take me to Heathrow, Sophie accompanied me, holding my hand. As I was put into the ambulance, I really felt as though my heart was breaking and I cried. The doors were closed and the ambulance pulled out into the London traffic. Keith observed, "There really seems to be something between Sophie and you." I said quietly, "Yes, there is."

As I felt a deep emptiness inside of me, I also feared that the previous six weeks were going to be easy compared with what lay ahead for me.

CHAPTER 5

Repatriation and Rehabilitation

Life became more difficult once I left my cocoon at St. Bartholomew's. The procedure for the repatriation was that a physician and a nurse licensed in the United States had to be brought to London to accompany me back on the airplane. I had to buy six airline seats, two of which were for me as their backs were folded down and a stretcher was bolted down over them. At Heathrow I entered side door towards the rear of the airplane on my stretcher by means of a lift and was carried flat on my back. It was late July, the height of the tourist season, and the plane was packed. Everyone in that section of the airplane turned to stare at me. I was transferred to the stretcher over the seats and connected to a heart monitor, as a precaution, and I still was catheterized. The only thing that made it bearable was that there was a C-shaped curtain encircling my seats and it shut out the rest of the cabin for me. Keith was with me, too, as were the physician and nurse, who had little to do except to be there should I have a problem during the journey.

The flight back to Chicago was hideous. I had lost so much weight that I was mostly bones on my backside and the stretcher was not generously padded. Within the narrow confines of the stretcher and tethered to heart monitor and catheter bag, I had little ability to adjust my position. I was nervous and apprehensive and I couldn't keep track of the time during the seemingly endless flight and, moreover, within my curtain shelter I had no diversions. I simply drifted in and out of sleep, constantly thinking back on all that had happened since I had flown over to England seven weeks earlier and pondering about what lay ahead. And I missed Sophie.

At last we approached Chicago and the plane landed at O'Hare. Indeed it really landed, for the plane smacked down on the runway with a hard thump which must have snapped heads forward, leaving the other passengers audibly gasping throughout the cabin. I was flat on my back on a minimally padded stretcher and I had almost no padding of my own to add for shock absorption. As we slammed down, the wind was knocked out of my lungs and I was literally gasping for air.

I exited the plane as I had entered it, by means of a lift raised up to the side of the plane, but at least this time I was the last off the plane and all those eyes that had stared at me before were now fixed on spotting their luggage and intent on making their way through customs. It was hot and steamy in Chicago in the middle of the terrible summer of 1988, very uncomfortable and such a contrast to the milder weather in London. Amazingly to me, the repatriation plans actually worked as planned. An ambulance really was waiting for me and whisked me off to Rush-Presbyterian-St. Luke's Medical Center in Chicago. I was admitted, taken to the pulmonary ward and placed in a room that happened to be equipped with a camera so I could be observed from the nurses' station. As soon as I was settled in my room, Keith took off for my apartment in Oak Park to get some rest.

I was home at last, alone in my room, which was the first time that I had really been entirely alone in six weeks. I missed my three companions in Radcliffe Ward and I longed to see Sophie, Sallie, Maura, Hazel, Andy, Jim and all the others back in London. They were all that I knew in this life of mine that had begun anew at St. Bartholomew's.

On the next day, Saturday, I awoke at 4 a.m., my body still on British time. I passed a few hours trying to channel the divine energy into my legs and especially into my still paralyzed left foot. About mid-morning I met the neurologist, Dr. Shannon, who came by to examine me, along with a group of residents. It was the usual neurological routine -- smile, try to resist my pressure, the key on the bottom of the foot. They all seemed amazed at my total lack of a reflex in my knees. Of course I was very thin (later I noticed that "severe malnutrition" had been written on my chart) and I still couldn't move my left foot. Dr. Shannon also ordered a bunny boot (something that looked like a large, padded ski boot) put on my legs, to try to prevent foot drop. Despite the good intentions I hated the monstrous looking thing for I couldn't move my foot at all in the boot and I was accustomed to focusing on any movement that I had and trying to expand it, which was impossible in the boot.

In addition, I was interviewed for possible admission into the hospital's new Rehabilitation Unit, which had opened only two weeks earlier. In that unit, I could receive more intensive physical therapy, twice a day rather than the usual once a day, and I could wear normal clothes instead of the charming, well ventilated regulation hospital gown. However, to be admitted, I had to have a condition that would probably profit from the intensive regime and I had to have a positive attitude that would make me a good recipient of the therapy. After all that had happened to me, the miracles that I had experienced, I was probably the most positive patient imaginable. This was far more important to me than my SATs and GREs had been and I passed the admissions requirements and was admitted into the Rehab Unit.

However, there was one sobering aspect to the interview. The physicians noted my very limited ability to move my feet. Not to worry, they assured me, there are a number of braces that I could be fitted with upon my discharge and I would be able to get around almost like normal. That was not much of a comfort because my ambitions were soaring and I was now greedy, wanting a life without such obvious signs of limitation. That afternoon, I was weighed. A big hoist-like apparatus was brought in to my room and a large piece of fabric was placed under me and connected to the hoist. I was lifted up, looking something like the picture of the baby being carried by the stork, and I weighed in at 146 lbs. That still was not very much but, on the positive side, I had probably put on ten or more pounds at St. Bartholomew's on my high calorie supplement and the generous eat-all-you-can-stuff-down diet.

On that first full day back in Chicago came one of the most worrisome events of my hospitalization. The catheter had to come out. In England there had been talk of beginning my retraining to use my bladder muscles—the process would be that the catheter would be clamped shut for a while and I would be able to start to feel the build up of urine, and then the period during which the catheter would be clamped off would gradually be extended. However, there had been so many distractions at Barts that they never quite got around to it. But now, at Rush, the catheter was simply removed all at once, with no retraining regime. For six weeks I had been blissfully unaware of the passage of any urine from my bladder through my urethra, and now, suddenly, I had to manage the urine flow on my own. I wasn't sure I could do it very well and I felt very close to panic. I tried to make myself aware of even the slightest hint of urine on its way out and for the next several nights I slept with a urinal in my hand just in case a sudden leak should take me unaware.

That night, alone in my room, I wanted to do something to work on my left foot, to get it to move, but while wearing the bunny boot I really couldn't move it at all. Back in my fuzzy memory I remembered reading about Chicago Bears quarterback Jim MacMahon's rehabilitation from shoulder surgery a few years earlier. His right arm was wrapped up and he couldn't move it but he began throwing footballs with his left arm. The rationale was that somehow exercising the good arm would help the bad one recover even though it was strapped down. (This is a phenomenon known as reciprocal innervation as I later learned from my friend Mary Lee Bergeron in Knoxville, who was a physical therapist.) It was certainly worth a try and I had nothing but time on my hands, so I began pushing against the foot of the bed with my right foot, hoping that somehow it would have a positive effect on the left.

On Sunday morning, I again awoke at 4 a.m., wide

awake with nothing to do. I was growing tired of the bunny boots, for they inhibited my exercising my feet and legs, and I took them off, hoping that Dr. Shannon would not find out. I then began visualizing the divine healing power flowing into my left foot and I pressed my bad left foot against the foot of my bed, pushing down with the leg. Then, around 6.30, I tried flexing the left foot, and it moved! In shock I continued flexing it. It moved, it actually moved -- another miracle on top of so many others.

I could now move everything and a crazy thought came to me. Perhaps I could stand up. Of course most of my muscles were destroyed and what remained had not been used in six weeks. I was so weak that I could scarcely hold a cup in my hand. Moreover, I was alone in my room and it was very early in the morning. What if I should fall? Ignoring all such rational and sensible thoughts, I decided to give it a try anyway. I threw my legs over the right side of the bed and stood up. I wobbled very badly, swaying forward and then back, but I remained standing. I could actually stand up!

I also got a good look at my body in the mirror opposite the bed. I was terribly thin and gaunt. I had almost no butt muscles at all, it was as if the gluteus maximus had become minimus. And yet, around the belly button, there was a little pocket of fat! That was really aggravating. In real life I would never be this thin, and if, after all that had happened, I still had fat on my stomach, there was no hope of ever getting rid of it. My legs quickly began to weaken, so I sat down on the bed. After a short rest, I stood up again. And I repeated this over and over until I began to feel stronger and more comfortable.

Now that I could stand up, I pushed on to new levels

of achievement and thought that I should give walking a try. I did realize that I could never do it on my own, for it was one thing to be lying down in bed and to move my legs, but to stand on my legs while they had to support my body's weight was impossible. I improvised a walker by pulling the tray stand over and adjusting it to the right height. I then leaned over it, put my weight on the tray and began pushing with my feet. I "walked" with the assistance of the tray over and over again, around the small open area in my room. This was fantastic. I wanted to let Sophie know that I had stood up and walked, at least sort of, in a day and a half rather than the two weeks that I had rashly vowed to her back in London.

But soon I grew very tired and had to sit back down on the bed and lie back for a rest. In a few minutes a nurse came into my room. Apparently she had been watching me on the television monitor. "Are you having some trouble walking?" she asked innocently. After all that had happened in the previous six weeks, I really didn't know to respond to such a question. Had she read my chart at all? I sighed and all I could say was, "Well, a little."

I was surprised when an Episcopal priest dropped by to see me. My friends in Tennessee, Paul and Mary Lee, had indeed responded with prayers when my brother called them from London at my request. Their priest had contacted the Episcopal Diocese of Chicago and a message was put through to Bishop Anderson House, which directs chaplaincy and pastoral care training in the Diocese of Chicago. The director of Bishop Anderson House, The Rev. Trenton Pitcher, came to see me a number of times before my release from the hospital and was a wonderful encouragement, especially as I pondered how to respond to my directive to go to the Episcopal Church. The new me was certain that I had to respond, but the old me was still wary of organized religion and leery of the whole enterprise.

On Monday I was taken to the Rehab Unit and joyfully I changed into my own clothes that my brother brought from my apartment. For the first time in six weeks, I wore real clothes. My roommate was a stroke victim who couldn't talk and it seemed that he could scarcely move. I wondered how he got here. Also in the unit were a young woman with Guillain-Barré Syndrome (that was supposed to be me, I thought, remembering the first diagnosis that I had received in London) and there was another woman with multiple sclerosis. She seemed to be in good spirits, but her mind had been affected by her disease and she tended to repeat herself when she talked. As I looked around, it seemed that we all were such sad cases.

In the afternoon I was to go down to the neurological department for my first EMG at Rush. When the wheelchair came to fetch me, I declined being carried to it, but insisted on displaying my new ability by walking over to the chair myself. It was a more of a lurch than a walk, but I did it myself. Walking that five feet or so without the assistance of my tray seemed to be the limit of my ability but I was extremely proud of it and I could ride the rest of the way in the wheelchair with a modicum of dignity and a sense of accomplishment. I was in for a long ordeal with the EMG. The neurologists there gave me a very thorough examination, from foot to eyebrow. The procedure is to place one electrode on one spot and another electrode on a different spot and then shoot a zap of electricity through the wires, measuring how long is required for the nerves to transmit the jolt from one electrode to the other. The zapping is mildly uncomfortable but I found the pressure they used to force the electrodes into my skin to be painful and uncomfortable, especially when they got up to my face and head and in particular to my eyebrows. And the zapping was more painful when it came to my face as well. This was not excruciating pain but it was strong and with the repeated EMGs I was given over the next few weeks, I had to get used to it. On the wall facing me in the EMG room was a picture of a forest scene and to take myself away from the pain I would visualize myself in the forest and try to lose myself in it, making imaginary journeys through the trees while the zapping was underway.

In the middle of the EMG, Dr. Shannon appeared to observe the tests. At the conclusion she said she would bring my wheelchair, about ten feet away, over for me. She was unaware of my new ability to lurch for a few feet for I had told no one about it. I said, "That's alright, I'll walk over to it myself." She arched her eyebrows at me in a highly skeptical look and said, "Go ahead and do it," and with a suspicious look on her face she stood back, arms crossed, to observe me. I swung my feet over the side of the bed, stood up, lurched over to the wheelchair and sat down. She had the most amazed look on her face. "What has happened?" she asked. "Just two days ago you could scarcely even move your legs." I told her the simple truth, "I got better."

That same day my mother arrived from Oklahoma. She was obviously relieved to see that I had progressed so well and that I was no longer in imminent danger of death. But I think that, in a sense, I looked too good, for she was no longer concerned that I was going to die or that I would be completely paralyzed for the rest of my life. She began to explain about all the expenses that she and Tullie had incurred while they were helping out my brother and sister and Tullie's son as well. After listing them all, she said that they were not going to pay for my repatriation as had been promised. I felt betrayed and I fumed, for this was not the first time something like this had happened in my family. Now I had no idea what I would do when that $10,000 American Express bill came. This was one more serious problem, the latest of so many, to deal with whenever I got out into the world. She did, however, offer to assist me in declaring bankruptcy, but I resented her limited help and was determined to handle this mess on my own.

Keith had gone to the post office that day and retrieved my mail that I had requested to be held for me. Of course that was when I had left for Europe back in early June when I thought that I would be away for two weeks. Now two months had passed and my affairs were very close to being in shambles as a number of second and third notices of past due bills were in the stacks of mail. My mother helped me sort through the bills and she wrote out the checks for me. I then had to sign the checks. My signature had not improved in the time since my experiments back at St. Bartholomew's a few days earlier, for I could barely hold the pen and my hand still shook rhythmically with a strong tremor as I wrote. I hoped no one at the bank would compare the signature on the checks with my signature on file, but at least the bills would be paid and I was spared complete financial collapse, at least for the present, until the American Express bill should arrive.

I did have some good discussions with Mother and surprisingly the historical information in my brain seemed to be mostly intact. How strange the memory is. My short-term memory was dreadful and I could remember very little from the three years before my illness, from the period 1985-1988. For that time I had only scattered pieces of memory and it was difficult for me to grasp entire events. An image came into my mind: my memory for those years was like a mirror that had been dropped, shattering into hundreds of pieces. Each piece had a clear picture in it but the pieces did not connect and form a coherent whole. Yet I could remember the historical information that I had worked so hard to gain. Where was that memory stored? How had it survived? I found that although my pre-1985 memories of my life were largely there, although there were many gaps, both large and small, they were different than they had been before my illness for they had almost no emotional content to them. My memories of my life were like a movie that I had watched countless times. I could relate the events and, at times, even recount the dialogue, but now they seemed in an odd way to have nothing to do with me. They were distant and I felt nothing for them. My past seemed entirely dead to me.

A social worker came to see me at Rush. I told her of my great concern for my memory, that I was still having trouble with short-term memory. She passed this on to the medical staff and before long I was given a memory and IQ test. I concentrated intently and in the end it was decided that, in general, I had no serious problem with my memory despite its gaps and holes that plagued me.

There was also concern about my voice, which was

very raspy and weak. The Ear, Nose and Throat people came by to see me and threaded their scope down my nose and throat to inspect my vocal chords as I made a variety of sounds as commanded. The verdict was that my vocal chords were indeed damaged, with some paralysis in them. I have since learned to live with a weak and reedy voice, much softer than it used to be, and I can't sing very much because it is hard for me to hit certain notes or to hold any of them.

Terri, the woman I had been dating until a few months before my illness, called me at the hospital. Someone from my department at the university, thinking that we were still dating, had notified her about my illness and impending death. So much had happened in the previous six weeks. Based on my revelation in my life review while I was in the Beyond, I told her that I now saw that she had been right most of the time, that I had been wrong, and that I was sorry. That was it. I think she was truly surprised for this was not like the old me. We had a long talk and the next day she came to visit me at the hospital. We talked for a long time and I told her of how I came to see things so differently, of how I had experienced things from her point of view. This was the one the first steps I had to take to rebuild my life on the basis of what I had experienced in the Beyond.

Dr. Shannon asked me if I would agree to appear at the Grand Rounds at Rush. As I understood it, it was something like a medical show and tell. Physicians presented their new and difficult cases to the others on the medical staff at the hospital, followed by a general discussion of the case. I agreed. I preferred to walk now that I could, but for a journey over some distance through the hospital's winding corridors I consented to ride in the wheelchair. I waited just outside the theater while she presented my case and then I was brought in. It seemed like perhaps there were a hundred people in attendance and of course they all had their eyes fixed on me. Dr. Shannon had me demonstrate my shuffling gait and then she described the tremendous loss of muscle mass and asked me to take off my shirt, which I did despite the small degree of embarrassment in revealing my emaciated body to the public. She then said I had to leave while they discussed the case. I thought this was very unfair. "I am not an idiot," I thought, "I have a PhD, I can follow conversations using big words and I am not likely to panic at anything I hear." Nothing that could be said would be more upsetting than when I was told that I probably would remain a quadriplegic the rest of my life. But I left quietly, not wanting to make a fuss.

For the next week and a half, my concentration was on physical therapy, which I began in earnest on Tuesday morning of week seven. It was not fun. I did whatever the therapist asked me to do, eager to cooperate fully. But she asked too much of my sad little muscle remnants and of my two-day-old walking ability. When I was supposed to go for the afternoon session on the first day, I found that I was completely exhausted, as every tiny muscle shred that remained to me, unaccustomed to doing very much work at all, now ached from deep within. I was unable to go to the afternoon session, which was a tremendous disappointment to me. However, I consoled myself with the memory that only one week earlier, I had been able to move only my left arm. I had come very far but all of this movement, especially standing and walking, which was vastly more tiring than scraping toast into my mouth, had drained me of energy in a way that I had never felt before. With more movement came more fatigue.

One major problem was my stance. I was proud that I could stand up, but apparently I had no muscle memory of how to stand properly. I was trying to keep my feet under my center of gravity, but the muscles keeping my torso straight were still very weak. The result was that I stood with my back curved into a kind of S-shape when viewed from the side. When I walked, I tried to keep my body carefully centered over my feet. I had forgotten that in walking one actually falls forward and sticks a foot out in front to catch the body. The therapist warned me that I had to work on a straighter stance and a better gait. I still tended to lurch around when I walked. Later I reflected that I must be one of the few people who can remember learning how to walk. I reminded myself of my son when he was taking his first steps as a baby, when we affectionately called him Lurch.

I did, however, find the therapist to be very irritating. In order to get my body into the desired position, she would simply shove my body around, which I found demeaning and infuriating. On the second day of therapy, I told her that we had to talk. I told her, "You have be more careful in asking me to do things in therapy, for I will try to do whatever you ask of me. But I am still very fragile and I don't think I should be driven to the point of exhaustion like yesterday." I added,"And I don't want you to push my body around. All you have to do is to tell me what you want me to do and I will try my best to do it. I want to be treated like a real person, not an object." She agreed to my requests and we got along fine from that point on.

For me the practice in walking was the most

important if I wished to resume anything like a normal life. I didn't like it that the therapist had to strap a very wide belt with handles on it around our waists. I knew that they had to be careful lest we fall, but I personally felt in no danger of falling and, for me, that belt was a presumption of incompetence. But rules were rules and the only way to get out of that belt was to graduate out of it, so I didn't fight her on the point.

My walking improved rapidly and, thanks to the therapist, I soon had something resembling a normal stance. My problem was stamina, for I tired extremely easily. By week eight, the second week at Rush, I could take small walks at night when the hospital was quiet and I could take my time without the fear being knocked down in crowded hallways. At first I was accompanied by one of the nurses on the Rehab Unit, but later I could shuffle along on my own. On one of my nocturnal walks I discovered the hospital chapel, which was cool, quiet and conducive to contemplation. Here, all alone, I could reflect on all that had happened to me in the past seven weeks and indeed in all my life. I thought about my direction to go to the Episcopal church and was apprehensive about returning to organized religion and unsure of what it would be like. I could meditate on my experience and revelations and ponder on how I was going to live in the future.

All in all, I found that physical therapy seemed to be intended for the mentally feeble. They talked to us in a condescending, slow-paced tone that is generally used for children and geriatrics who can't hear or follow a conversation. Especially unpleasant were Saturday mornings. Apparently state law mandated a certain amount of "recreation therapy," so all of us in the Rehab Unit were gathered together to go bowling. Very large and light-weight plastic bowling pins were set up at one end of the occupational therapy room and an equally light-weight plastic bowling ball was on the floor at the other end. In almost complete silence we watched each other roll the ball down the floor into the pins. How exciting. My roommate, the stroke victim, could scarcely move his arm, much less roll the ball. But, wheelchair bound as he was, he was required to give it a try even though the pins were in no danger of actually being touched by the ball, which would just fall out of his hand and lazily roll a meandering path until it came to rest a few feet away from him. After we each had about three rolls of the ball, we could go back to our rooms. I could not imagine what this was supposed to accomplish other than allowing the hospital to comply with the law. I found it demeaning and none of us seemed to view the experience as recreation.

It was fascinating to watch my fellow patients. We members of the Rehab Unit had our physical therapy in the same room and at the same time as the outpatients and other inpatients did but of course we were there twice each day. I noticed many different attitudes and approaches towards the physical rehabilitation as well as towards illness, injury and disability. There was one young man, perhaps in his mid-twenties, who was a double amputee, just below the knees. As he pushed himself along in his wheelchair he reeked of self-pity. He came up to a young man who looked to be sixteen or so, with a massive cast on his right leg that was slung in a support apparatus. Obviously he had undergone some very serious surgery. Without any prompting, the amputee spoke to him and said, "You think you've got it bad, don't you? How would you like to be like me?" I remembered back a week and a half earlier (was it really only a week and a half ago? It seemed as though months had passed). As I lay in Bart's as a quadriplegic I would have envied the amputee and his mobility. I guess illness, disability and injury are relative.

There was a young woman, around twenty, with an ugly, fresh surgical scar on her left knee and seemed unenthusiastic about physical therapy. Her mother was always with her, imploring her to keep trying despite the pain. "You can't get better if you dont exercise your leg," she kept pleading to her, but her daughter was always pouty, reluctant and balky. An older man around the age of sixty had a hip replacement and he threw himself into the exercise with energy and determination. Naturally I thought that I was the model patient, but it was a fact that I was eager to do everything I could to gain control of my body and strengthen the remnants of my muscles.

Practice going up and down stairs was important but it was also extremely tiring for me. While my muscles were getting better and walking, my quadriceps had great difficulty lifting my entire body. At some point back at St. Bartholomew's I had been told that the quadriceps were the first to go and the last to return. How true it was. In the hallway there was a simple little device, three or four steps up to a platform and then three or four steps down. As simple as it was, it was intimidating and I always approached it as a personal challenge. They taught us a little phrase, "To heaven with the good, to hell with the bad," meaning that when ascending steps, the stronger leg should go first but when descending, the weaker should lead the way as the stronger provided support and balance. It was an exhausting challenge to make it up and down those few little steps. Life on the outside seemed unimaginable to me.

With my mobility, I discovered secondary physical problems. One nuisance was due to the fact that in paralysis, the connective tissue between skin and muscle, the superficial fascia, hardens. I now had hardened fasciatic tissue in the webbing of my hands, between the thumbs and index fingers, and on the soles of my feet. The only remedy is to massage them out but I was so weak in my hands that I could make little progress on those hard knots. I had to rely on the kindness of others, especially the occupational therapist. I also had some odd "holes" in some of my muscles, depressions in the midst of the muscles, especially below my ankles and in the back of my hands, where the muscles had atrophied.

I also discovered the cause of the sensation of pins sticking me in my left thigh when I had been placed on the tilting table at St. Bartholomew's. Dr. Shannon told me that I had lost so much weight that the nerve running down the outside of my left leg had left its track and when my knee was moved, as when I was put in the "frog position," the bones were grinding on the nerve. The damage was in the knee area, but the pain was manifested in the thigh. I also had a very numb patch, quite painful to the touch, covering most of the left thigh. But there was more. Just inside the front of my left hip bone was extremely sensitive. It reminded me of the hip-pointer that I had suffered when I played football in high school. Now that I was moving around, I discovered that the spot reacted badly when I twisted or turned and it definitely did not like being touched. Dr. Shannon said that it was similar to the injuries suffered by workmen who have to wear heavy belts around their waists, such as toolbelts. It, too, was due to the weight loss that allowed the nerve to stray from its usual spot.

To me, one of the worst aspects of my paralysis had been my inability to clip my own fingernails. They had grown quite long during my stay at St. Bartholomew's. My brother had tried to clip them for me while we were there, but his efforts gave me the impression that he was trying to shoe a horse. The angle of the clipper on my nails was terrible and he seemed to cut into the skin and the quick more than he trimmed the nails. But now, at Rush, I had regained use of both my hands so I decided to have a go at it. I carefully placed the clippers on my nail in just the right position and squeezed. Nothing happened. I squeezed again and again nothing happened. I didn't have the strength in my hands to move the clippers through the nail. Reluctantly I had to ask my mother to clip them. She was a little better at it than Keith had been, but only a little. In Occupational Therapy in the Rehab Unit I wanted them to show me how I could do it but they had no ideas. I worked on it and at last found a solution. If I positioned the clipper only at the very edge of the nail, I could make a little nick in the nail. Then I moved the clipper into the nick and moved it slightly farther across the nail and squeezed, and the nick broadened. Methodically and with determination I worked my way across the nail. At last it was done. Another triumph, and I moved on to the next nail. Exultantly I told the occupational therapist of my technique but she was entirely unimpressed and acted as though I might have a problem with my nail obsession.

My triumph was tarnished—instead of being clever, I was obsessive. However, I thought that if they truly wished to return patients into the world able to lead independent lives, the ability to clip one's own nails is not a minor skill. Often the quality of life depends on simple little matters like one's nails.

During those two weeks at Rush, I had a series of EMGs. Dr. Shannon had left the hospital at the end of week seven to start her vacation, to visit the Gilroy, California, Garlic festival as I recall (I remember thinking, "Garlic for a vacation?"), and now Dr. Aaron Buchman was in charge of my neurological testing. It seemed as though I was having another EMG virtually every other day. Dr. Buchman told me that he had never seen or heard of the kind of condition I was in. He said that there was nerve damage from my eyebrows down to my feet. Sometimes the damage was to the nerve fibers, at other times to the sheaths, and the damage was spotty and erratic, lacking any recognizable pattern. Moreover, my pattern of recovery was erratic as well. First the left arm moved, then the right leg, then the right arm and finally the left leg. From beginning to end the whole thing was a mystery to him. He told me that he would like to stay on the case and if my insurance would not pay for me to see him, he would like to see me anyway, at no charge.

By Friday, August 5, 1988, I was ready to go home. It was now week eight of my illness. Seven weeks and two days, fifty-one days in all, had passed since my arrival at the emergency room at St. Bartholomew's hospital. It had been six weeks since I had regained full consciousness that I could remember, when I learned that my paralysis might be forever. It was twelve days after I stood up. Moreover, I had the distinction of being the first patient to graduate from the newly opened Rehab Unit. My progress had surpassed even my buoyant hopes that I expressed to Sophie when I was leaving St. Bartholomew's. I couldn't wait to let her know how things had turned out.

I now weighed a whopping 155 pounds, ten pounds more than when I had arrived at Rush-Presbyterian less than two weeks earlier, but I was still concerned about my lack of muscle mass. While I could walk, now with something close to proper posture, thanks to physical therapy, I could not walk very far without great fatigue. Much more physical therapy was going to be needed to rebuild my muscles and to gain greater control over them. Moreover, I was concerned about simply taking care of myself.

But there was a deeper problem. Due to my experience while I was off in the Beyond, I had a profound rejection of my own life. I did not want to return to any part of it. I didn't want to set foot in my apartment. I didn't want to return to my teaching, which I now saw as being rather pointless. What difference did it really make that my students might gain a proper understanding of the Roman constitution or of the causes of the Crusades? I wanted to do something important with my life but, unfortunately, I didn't know what that might be and meanwhile I still had to make a living and I had two children to help take care of. I was about to be on my own and there was so much to do. I had to rebuild my body, rebuild my mind, rebuild my soul, rebuild my life. That was all.

I was ready to walk out of the hospital under my own steam. As I was leaving the hospital, I had a final meeting with Dr. Buchman. He wanted to tell me the results of my latest EMG. He laughed and said, "You dont know it, but you can't walk. The EMG shows perhaps some marginal improvement in nerve conductivity, but nothing that reflects the actual physical improvement that we see. Your nerves are not conducting electrical impulses well enough to allow you to walk." How odd. I knew that miracles had occurred as I regained movement and I assumed that whatever had been damaged was now fixed. But this was different. It wasn't as though first there was this massive damage to my nerve fibers and I was paralyzed, and then miraculously the damage was healed and now I could move. The damage was still there and yet I could move, I could walk, in spite of it. What was all this about?

Now it was time to see what awaited me out in the world.

CHAPTER 6

Life Begins Anew

I was both eager to leave my two-month-long existence of hospital living and dreading my return to "normal" life. Those two months had been crammed with the most sublime experiences possible for humans, the most agonizing pain imaginable, the worst challenge of my life and the most incredible miracles. There had been one challenge after another that I had to overcome—surviving my illness, regaining a clear mind, working to regain movement, struggling to pass my pulmonary exams, the flight home, standing up at Rush-Presbyterian and the rapid progress through the Rehab Unit. I had met the most wonderful people in the world, owed my life to most of them, and felt deeply attached to two of them. Now I was returning to my own world, mostly alone. It would be a more routine existence with few dramatic hurdles to clear, but instead progress was going to be measured in tiny, almost imperceptible increments.

After leaving the hospital and approaching my apartment, a sense of near panic rose inside of me and my heart began pounding in my chest. Slowly and tentatively I dragged myself to my door and unlocked it, and, after an absence of two months, I entered my apartment. It was both familiar and foreign to me. It was strange and empty and alien, a part of a past that I now rejected. But it was worse than that. I went to my closet and opened the doors to put my things away and looked at my clothes in disbelief. I hated them! They were boring. What idiot had picked them out?

Even though I was dreading the arrival of the American Express bill for my repatriation and I still had no idea how I was going to pay it, I had to make one major purchase immediately. The heat of the summer of 1988 was still oppressing Chicago, killing hundreds of people, and I had no air conditioning in my apartment. In my frail condition and with my still fragile lungs, it was vital that I be out of that heat. It was very late in the season to be buying an air conditioner and only one remained at the store, and that one with a damaged front, a feature that did at least save me a few dollars on the price. Unfortunately the unit was also extremely heavy while I was barely able to grasp a doorknob hard enough to turn it. When I asked the clerk if someone could please carry it to the car and lift it in, he gave me a long, hard look, as though I were a real wimp. When I returned home, my neighbor Ken Kane, who lived with his wife Deborah at the other end of the apartment building from me, was a real friend in the time of my need and cheerfully lugged the air conditioner into my apartment and even installed it in the window for me. Once again I was very grateful for others' generosity that seemed to appear when I was so helpless.

Now that I was back in the real world, I began to learn about life as a partially disabled person. The first awakening I had was how incredibly heavy everything was. To open most doors, and virtually all of those at the university, I would have to grasp the handles with both hands and pull with all my strength. To pick up a gallon of milk required my full effort and both of my hands. A friend of mine was amused as I told her about this new perspective on life and she said, "Now you know what it is like to be female." I found that my hands were too weak to hold the briefcase that I would carry to work, so I had to buy a new bag, one with a shoulder strap.

To drive my car, both hands were needed to turn the steering wheel and it was all I could do to push down the clutch with my very weak left leg. I felt as though I were driving a huge bus instead of my little Mustang. To build up my stamina I tried walking as much as I could, but I was not a pretty sight, for I had a severe limp in my left foot. I shuffled along, unable to lift my feet up very high, with my left foot flapping off to the side, making a slapping sound as it whacked against the pavement. And I was slow, very slow. I discovered that I couldn't cross a street at a traffic signal before the light changed from green to red again, leaving me stranded in the crosswalk blocking the drivers in their cars who were in a hurry to be on their way. "Be patient with me, I'm really trying my best," I thought as the irritated drivers suffered through my efforts to shuffle out of the crosswalk.

I had about a month before the start of the Fall Quarter at the university, one month to build up my body enough to walk from my apartment to the elevated train stop (mercifully only one block distant from my apartment), and from the university "el" stop to my office, to teach my classes, and then to repeat the journey back home. The HMO had approved outpatient physical therapy for me, but only for three weeks. The problem was that there was no one area of my body to concentrate on, for every muscle of my body needed therapy. I did the exercises prescribed for me by the therapist and on my own I also decided that yoga exercises would be best for me because they would work all my muscles. The physical therapy, however, was not easy. To get back to Rush-Presbyterian, I would have to wrestle with my car to drive the eight miles or so to the hospital and park in the garage. I would then shuffle up the inclined ramp to the hospital entrance and make my way through the winding corridors until I arrived at physical therapy, exhausted at the effort simply to get there and almost too drained to begin my exercises.

Just before my discharge from Rush I had asked my physician about getting a handicapped parking badge so that I could park in those handicapped spaces so wonderfully near the doors of most businesses as well as the entrance to the hospital. "Sorry," she said, "but you're not in bad enough shape to qualify." I found that difficult to believe then, and now as I was shuffling my way up the ramp of Rush and passing by all those dedicated handicapped parking spaces, I never saw anyone get in or out of the cars parked there whom I could have beaten in a race or even in a walk. They all seemed to be moving perfectly fine to me, and it seemed that something was wrong with the system. But I continued my trek up the parking ramp, counting it as part of my physical therapy.

My feet continued to be two very painful problems. They were no longer the painful sausages that they had been in London, but they still ached constantly. My leg muscles were not very good at assisting the pumping of the blood back up to the rest of my body, so if I stood on my feet for very long, my feet and ankles would begin to swell, at times looking like over-inflated balloons pouring over the sides of my shoes and hurting like hell. In general, I found that my feet were extremely sensitive and almost all shoes that I already had hurt them far too much for me to tolerate. I ended up buying three new pairs of shoes before I found a pair that I could wear for any extended period. I found it odd that my feet could hurt so much and still have so little feeling in them. They were not entirely numb but almost so. I could feel them but the sensation of touch was so muted that it was as if I were wearing about seven pairs of socks over them.

The next month was a blur. I tired incredibly easily. I did my exercises and then slept, I went for a short walk and then slept, I went to the store for food and then slept. There was also another urgency that I felt in this month. As soon as my right hand recovered strength and the tremor disappeared, I began writing down my experiences at St. Bartholomew's and at Rush-Presbyterian. I wanted to remember all that had happened to me and the people who had made such a difference in my life—Sally, Sophie and all of the hospital staff at Barts, the dreams, hallucinations, visions and understandings that had come to me, my own self-judgment in its full harshness, the progress of my miraculous recovery of movement. This effort to capture my memories grew to become almost daily journaling for the next several years.

As soon as I was able, I did as Sally had asked me when she left for her holiday when I was at St. Bartholomew's, I wrote her at the hospital and told her of my astounding physical progress. When she had left, I was almost completely paralyzed and now I was out of hospital, walking around. For several months I heard nothing in return from her, which was a disappointment, for I still felt so strongly for her. Then, surprisingly, after about six months, a letter from her arrived, expressing her delight at my physical recovery. She had been experiencing a number of changes in her own life, including having left St. Bartholomew's to become a ward sister at another hospital in London, and she had quite understandably been rather distracted. However, by now I knew that I would be returning to England in the following April in order to deliver a paper at a scholarly conference, this time in Sheffield, and we made arrangements for us to meet while I was there.

I was also relieved that my relationship with Sophie had not come to an end. She was back at her university studies in Bath and we wrote frequently and even talked on the telephone a few times. The affection that had been between us when I had left England seemed to have persisted as strongly as possible considering the separation of time and space and we also agreed to see each other again when I made my return to England in April.

By the time that school started up again in late mid-September, my body had gained sufficient strength for me to teach my classes. However going to the university and teaching my classes were a terrible drain on my energy. I would haul my body up to the el and then to work. I taught my classes, stayed around for my office hours and committee meetings and then would leave as soon as I could. After hauling my body back home I would collapse and nap. On days that I didn't have classes to teach, I stayed home and napped. For the rest of that Fall term, my life seemed to consist of teaching, sleeping and exercising when I could find the time and marshal the energy. I got a view of how I appeared to my ten-year-old daughter during this period when she showed me an essay she wrote in school on "my favorite person," which was about me. She concluded her essay, "The reason I couldn't live without him is because he's my favorite person in my family. He's barely ever mean but sometimes he's tired because he had an asthma attack about 5 months ago. Other than that he's usually awake and lots of fun, and energetic!"

Despite my fatigue at having to function in the world, my physical strength continued to improve but not always as much as I imagined. One morning as I was going through the turnstile at the el stop I heard the sound of my train arriving at the station and I knew that I would have to hurry in order to make it. As I would have done any previous time, I rushed to the stairs and began running up them. My mind had my legs chugging along in high gear, but my legs were actually dragging behind in low gear. I was simply plodding up the stairs. Stairs were the worst for my legs, with serious damage to the quadriceps remaining. It felt as though I were trying to run in knee-deep water.

In October I thought it was time to take the air conditioner out of the window for winter and by now I was so confident of my increasing strength that I decided not to call upon Ken's good will again but to take it out myself. I stood at the window with a chair behind me on which I could place the air conditioner once it was removed, for I knew that I probably could not hold it in my hands very long. I removed the screws holding the unit in place and then gave it a good tug. It started coming out of the window and then to my horror I realized that I didn't have the strength to stop it or even to lift it. Gravity and momentum pulled it out of the window and it smashed against my right leg, knocking me against the chair behind me. The air conditioner was gouging into my leg and at the same time I felt that my leg might break from being pressed against the chair at an odd angle, but I couldn't budge the air conditioner when I tried to lift it. I felt as though I were caught in a bear trap and I was there in my apartment all alone, far from the phone. I had to endure the double pain in my leg and control my panic instinct while I concentrated on breathing exercises to regain my composure and to regain strength in my arms and hands. After a few minutes I tried to pull up into my arms all the strength in my body and with a great surge of energy I was able to swing the air conditioner off my leg and on to the chair. I was saved. After resting again to regain my strength, I left the air conditioner perched on the chair, which I then pushed across the floor and into a closet. I closed the door and left them both, chair and air conditioner, right where they were during the winter and the next spring.

I also continued to be faced with the fact that my short-term memory was porous. My long-term memory seemed to be relatively good, again except for the period 1985-1988, the years for which I had only scattered memories. Sometimes I felt as though a clear memory were right in the front of my brain, ready to pop out, but it often would remain in place, elusive and evading my consciousness. My mouth would be open, ready to say something but nothing would come out. It was the oddest thing. However, it was a relief that most of the historical information was still up there so I could continue to do as I had for many years, lecturing in my classes essentially without the aid of my notes. Nonetheless, my bad short-term memory was a constant problem. I often found myself at the university library, standing there, without a clue as to why I had gone there. This was extremely aggravating as well as frightening, and after about the third time this happened, tears came to my eyes out of sheer frustration. One day I took my daughter to a music store to get a cassette that I promised to buy for her. After we looked around for a while and we were ready to leave, I told her to go get the tape so I could pay for it. She gave me one of those looks and said, very slowly and distinctly, "It's in ... your hand." I looked down. There it was. I couldn't remember how it had gotten there.

In the end I had to take measures to deal with the problem. First I tried writing notes about things that I needed to remember, but then I wouldn't remember that I had written the notes so the technique proved largely ineffective. Eventually I had to try to make myself do something the instant I thought of it. If I needed to take something to school with me, I would place it against my front door so I would trip over it as I left for work. I even adopted a technique my daughter used, writing reminders on my hand.

I also found one great advantage in having a poor memory. Not long after I was released from the hospital, I was talking with Terri, the woman I dated for three years, up until a few months before my illness, and I told her, "I know that I am supposed to be mad at you about something, but I can't remember what it is. All I can do is forget about it." It made me think that perhaps it was a good thing not to be able to remember every little detail of some events. I had come to realize that my memory had really been a curse at times, for I could get too caught up in who was right or wrong and exactly what it was that someone had said or done. I seemed to be able to remember every slight and not let it go. I now thought that perhaps I could be a better person if I didn't remember so much.

A few months after my return, the dreaded American Express bill appeared. The delay was so long that I began to believe that perhaps another miracle had been worked on my behalf, that the charge had somehow been lost and I would never have to deal with it. But reality returned when it did come, leaving me with about a month to come up with either the money or a plan. I did have a small sum of money left to me by my grandfather when he died, but that would cover less than half of what was owed. My fretting reached a new intensity and then suddenly it hit me—I had two modest life insurance policies that I had owned for several years and they had some cash value, maybe enough to cover what I was short. When I called the insurance company to terminate the policies they told me that I didn't need to cancel the policies for I could borrow their cash value, at very low interest, and in fact I did not actually have to repay the loan. When the time came for the policies to be redeemed, any unpaid loans would simply be subtracted from the final payment. I was able to borrow about $4000 on the policies, but still I didn't quite have the payment to American Express. I looked at my checking account, and to my relief I had just enough of a financial cushion there to make up the missing amount.

I sent the check off to American Express, simply glad to have survived the crisis, and then I surveyed my financial situation. My savings account had been wiped out. I had always thought of it as being there for a rainy day, but when the rainy day actually came, it really annoyed me to have to use it for that purpose. I was now in debt, sort of, to the insurance company, I had a substantial credit card bill from the purchases that were necessary upon my return, my checking account held the grand sum of fifty dollars and I had a few other stray dollars in my wallet and some pocket change. That was it, with no hope of any cash infusion before my next paycheck came in two weeks. For the next fourteen days I hunkered down, spent money only on what I absolutely had to have (necessary groceries and only enough gasoline to make sure I didn't run dry while driving) and was unable to pay any new bills that came in until the first of the month. My kids started asking why suddenly we couldn't go to MacDonald's or Long John Silver's anymore. The next few months were fairly scary until I was able to build up a bit of a reserve again, but at least I had paid my American Express bill, I hadn't gone into bankruptcy and I had done it on my own. One more crisis managed, just barely.

The winter months gave me a new challenge, as my old Ford Mustang kept dying on me. Each time I would have to call a tow truck and have to pay what now, in my financial hardship, seemed to be an outrageous fee to take it to the mechanic's. Now I certainly couldn't afford anything but patch-up repairs and while the car was being worked on I was literally on foot in the snow and cold at a time when I was still very physically weak and my feet were painful and uncoordinated. When the car died the third time, in January, the worst point in the Chicago winter, I began crying in exasperation, "Not again, not again!" And then it hit me, "Oh come on," I scolded myself, "when you were paralyzed in London this would not have seemed like such a severe problem to have to face. All you have to do is call the tow truck again, the car will be repaired, you'll pay for it somehow."

* * *

While I was working at rehabilitating my body, I also had to get to work at the rest of my rebuilding program. One of the things I did was to resume meditation, which always seems so natural when one is doing yoga. I would usually burn a candle to serve as a point of concentration and in time I was meditating for an hour or more. As sometimes happens in meditation, however, I was unable to get my mind away from the flow of mundane and distracting thoughts which seemed to parade through my mind unbidden and unwanted but unstoppable. During these times I tried to keep in mind the Zen saying, "sit just to sit," that is, sit in meditation without expectations of results. At other times, however, I felt that I could connect with another reality and I gained significant insight into what I should be doing. In my journal I wrote: *At this moment I feel as though I have for the moment broken through the thin barrier into eternity and grasped truth, the truth that all will be well. There is no cause for worry or anguish. No need to try to manage everything. I can just relax and enjoy life. I am doing enough.*

Throughout this time, I was constantly aware of the presence of something constantly with me, ever comforting me through my difficulties. Perhaps it was the Being who was with me in the Beyond, for there was the same feeling of immensity about it. If I close my eyes I can recall the vivid, hyper-real memories of my experiences there. It was a constant reminder of what I had experienced and what I had been through.

Thus I knew that I had to go to the Episcopal church, for never for a moment did I consider ignoring this direction that had been given to me so clearly at St. Bartholomew's. I started attending St. Christopher's Episcopal Church without knowing exactly what it was that I was supposed to do there, for the direction was simply to go, but I felt I should become as involved as I could and they would allow. I also felt that I was there to learn, not to teach, for I knew so well that I knew nothing and that I had everything to learn.

Any doubts that I might have had were shattered that first Sunday when the priest began saying Mass. He got to the elevation of the host and he raised high the large wafer, the priest's host, which is about the diameter of a rice cake. He grasped it in both hands, with thumbs together facing him and his index and second fingers placed together facing us. He snapped the host in half, vertically. He then put the two pieces back together and raised them up facing us. "The gifts of God for the people of God," he said, and then he broke the two halves into many other pieces and placed them on the paten, the small plate on the altar before him. Chills ran down my neck and over my shoulders. This was the vision I had at St. Bartholomew's, of Maura Falvey (the de Boers twin) holding the golden, glowing rice cake, asking me if I wanted it, telling me that it was for me, and then breaking it into many pieces before she put into my respirator. This scene seemed to confirm that indeed I was supposed to be here. I decided that I would stay here.

I was puzzled that I could not bring myself to take communion even though it was stated clearly on the bulletin that it was open to all baptized Christians. I had been thoroughly baptized, twice, once in the Church of Christ and a second time as a Catholic. But I couldn't bring myself to take communion. I knew so well how unworthy I was, what a failure I was, and I did believe firmly that the bread and wine were the body and blood of Christ. But I didn't believe that Christ was confined to those elements, for I believe that God is everywhere and in everything. Indeed I felt that I was constantly in the presence of God. But to me it seems that we are too blind to the important realities of life to realize this so we need a special occasion to make it obvious to us. The Eucharist, or communion, or Lord's Supper or Mass, is the vehicle for that awareness. I believe that whenever we breathe we take God into us, whenever we eat or drink, we take God into us. But the Eucharist is a special form, something we do consciously with full awareness. But I couldn't take communion, not in my state. As I got to know the priest, he asked me why I was not taking communion and I told him about my feelings of unworthiness. He gave me his best counseling, but it was of no use. Moreover, I could not count myself an Episcopalian yet. I needed to know more about the Episcopal church.

I attended a newcomers' class, taught by the priest with the assistance of a layman. Due to my historical studies and my fundamentalist upbringing I already knew a great deal about the Bible, about general church history, and even much about Anglican history, so the course went fairly rapidly. The priest was showing me around the Book of Common Prayer, of which I knew very little. He started with the Daily Office in the front of the Prayer Book and stated that many Episcopalians said the Daily Office as part of their spiritual life. I thought the implication was that this was something that "good Episcopalians" did, so I then began the daily ritual of saying Morning and Evening Prayer by myself and reading the scripture readings specified for each day.

One day I was browsing through the tract rack and a pamphlet caught my eye. It was on the Episcopal church, stating that the Episcopal church can not tell people what their relationship with God is supposed to be like, but it is there to help them work out this relationship for themselves. Maybe this was why I was sent to the Episcopal Church. A non-dogmatic church trying to help me find God, not preaching to me with its own ideas on the subject! I liked this.

My body continued to recover and I was putting on weight and building up my muscle strength. I was going to the Episcopal church. I was attempting to reestablish my life on a different basis, one that I wouldn't mind re-experiencing the next time I died. I had to remake myself and I needed to be alone to do it. I had to heal my wounds and break my habits. I had to cease needing a romantic relationship, which would be possible only if I were not involved with anyone and learned the difference between being alone and being lonely. I needed to learn to enjoy being alone so I decided to isolate myself as much as possible and incorporate all that I had experienced into my nature, to make myself over into a different person, one who could lead the kind of life that I now knew about.

As Thanksgiving neared I was still unable to take the

Eucharist and the priest suggested that perhaps it would help if I made a confession, which initially scared me, but soon I felt that it was worth a try. But I would have so much to confess, in fact, my entire life, it seemed to me, but soon I realized that was ridiculous. I should only confess the matters that were really on my mind. We set a date and I began to prepare myself. But then, the problem cleared up in a flash of understanding. One of the scripture readings that week was on the prodigal son and, as it was being read, insight began to pour into my mind. Even the prodigal son was forgivable. No one was unforgivable. Why was my ego acting up again, making my faults so damned heinous that I, I, was unforgivable? What made me think that I was so special? Some people just never learn. My ego was rearing up under the guise of humility. So I went down the next Sunday and took the Eucharist, to the priests clear surprise. Afterwards, we talked about it and I agreed with the priest that it was probably a good idea that I go ahead with the confession anyway, and so it was done.

The entire experience taught me something of the importance of confession. It is one thing to believe that you have done something wrong. However, it could be that we guard that realization and keep it private. Outwardly we can still be in denial and not really face up to our faults. But to make a good confession is to name our fault and to tell it to another person. It is to be truly sorry for what we have done and to have every intention of correcting it, it is to face up to our failings and acknowledge them.

Quite often during the eucharistic service I would feel that I was shifting out of this present reality and into a different one although it was very near to the one in which I had been. The scene in front of me would seem to shimmer and a feeling of great distance between me and everything around me would set in. It was as if my consciousness had moved into a new existence although my body was still standing in the old. I would feel caught between the two worlds. And then the shimmering would slowly fade away and I felt back into this standard reality in which we live. Oddly, the entire experience seemed perfectly normal. I think that after all that I had experienced the criteria for what constituted the strange had been significantly loosened.

The Eucharist became the most important part of church for me. It is was the fulfillment of the words, "God in me." As the priest would say the Eucharistic prayer with the chalice of wine resting on the altar, often I would feel myself actually in that chalice as well, at one with the wine that was Christ. The part that ended the Eucharistic prayer, the one concluded by the congregation's affirmation of "Amen," was special, "By him, and in him, and with him, in the unity of the Holy Spirit, now and forever." To me, it was the reminder that God is always with us and in us as well as a reminder of my vision of the golden rice cake.

I wanted the Eucharist as much as possible, so I started attending the Tuesday evening service at St. Christopher's, which was also the healing service at the parish, at which the priest would invite those who wished to come forward for the laying on of hands. I was reluctant to go forward, even though I certainly had enough physical problems to keep him busy anointing me. Especially evident was the damage to my legs, now that I was taking the Eucharist and kneeling at the altar rail to receive it. My quadriceps were badly damaged in my illness and it was an ordeal to lower myself down to the kneelers and even more of one to raise myself up again. It was slow and painful. The priest suggested that I remain standing but to me it was important to kneel. The pain didn't matter.

I had a definite idea about pain. It was therapeutic, it was my penance, and I had now come to see the wisdom in it. If we know that we have done wrong, it is easier to move past it if we make amends somehow. That allows us to "make it up." We have done wrong, but when we pay a penalty for it, we are even in the great scheme of life and we can move on. The penance is not a punishment, but instead it is a psychological making of amends that evens things up and allows us not to carry guilt around with us. I also came to believe that we only learn through pain. Without pain, whether mental or physical, we are complaisant and not very inclined to make changes. The pain teaches us that we need to change. I had lots of pain remaining, especially in my feet and legs. The quadriceps hurt when they were used and the numb patch on my left thigh still was extremely sensitive to the touch. But I also felt that pain was my friend, telling me what no one else could, that I needed to change.

As Christmas approached, a familiar feeling began nagging at me. December 22 was nearing, the anniversary of the death of my father, exactly twenty years earlier in 1968. It was on a Thursday this year and I felt that I needed to go to church that day, but there was no Thursday service at St Christopher's, but I knew that the other Episcopal church in Oak Park, Grace Church, had a Thursday night healing service. I decided to attend, just for that night, so that I could take the Eucharist. I walked in to the unfamiliar chapel in the unfamiliar church and perhaps ten people were there.

The priest was Fr. John Seville, the interim priest while the parish was searching for a new rector. I loved the service, so plain, simple and straightforward, and the people there were also very welcoming. I had intended only to go there for that one service, for I already had a church home at St. Christopher's. However, I enjoyed the service so much that I decided to go back the next Thursday night as well, and then the following Thursday, too, and soon I was attending virtually every week. Now I was attending three Eucharistic services each week -- Sunday morning and Tuesday evening at St. Christopher's, and Thursday evening at Grace Church. I was saying the Daily Office, both Morning and Evening Prayer, as well and I was loving the whole experience.

It was at about this time that I discovered that I must have unwittingly become an Episcopalian. One day as I was leaving the Sunday service at St. Christopher's, I glanced at the table at the back of the church and saw a box of pledge envelopes resting there, and across the label I noticed my name on it. I guessed that it meant that I was now a member there, but there wasn't much fanfare to the whole thing, I thought. I picked up the box and carried it away with me, now an Episcopalian.

At church, I found a friend, Bill. He was a small, frail-looking man, with a moustache and stooped stance, who walked as if he might break, but he called himself "Wild Bill." Bill started sitting by me and while I appreciated the friend, I wasn't sure about how close I wanted to get to him. I am not one of those people who can spot a gay man right off, but even to me he seemed gay. Being new at this church, did I want people to think that I was gay? I pondered this dilemma briefly and finally decided, "What the Hell," and I accepted the friendship that he was offering and I valued it.

Bill was a liturgical purist. Nobody could cross himself or bow or kneel more than Bill did. For a newcomer to the Episcopal church like myself, this was an invaluable lesson in the secrets of Episcopal liturgy. At first I had found it difficult to balance the Book of Common Prayer on one knee and the hymnal on the other. Moreover, there were many options in the Prayer Book and initially I couldn't figure them out. I would look around me to see what others were doing, but half the people seemed not to be looking at the prayer book at all, saying everything from memory. I did not have to bow, cross and kneel as Bill did, but at least I knew when I could if I wanted to. Bill explained to me what was happening during the liturgy and how it corresponded to the directions and options in the Prayer Book.

Ash Wednesday and the Lenten season approached, the beginning of my first Easter season as an Episcopalian. The Ash Wednesday service started early in the morning at St. Christopher's with perhaps fifteen people in attendance. We moved into the litany of penance and began our collective confession to God. We confessed the basics, "We have not loved you with our whole heart, and mind, and strength. We have not loved our neighbors as ourselves. We have not forgiven others as we have been forgiven. ... We have been deaf to your call to serve ... we have grieved your Holy Spirit." We confessed "the pride, hypocrisy, and impatience of our lives," and then it began to become personal, not general. I saw myself in those words and I began to feel a heaviness in my chest. We confessed "our indulgent appetites and ways, and our exploitation of other people." This, too, was true for me individually and the heaviness pressed down on me more strongly. We continued to confess, "our anger at our own frustration, and our envy of those more fortunate than ourselves, ... our dishonesty in daily life and work," and those words continued to describe me and burn into me. I had seen during my life review that all of this was true. The litany moved on, as we asked that our repentance be accepted "for the wrongs that we have done: for our blindness to human need and suffering, and our indifference to injustice and cruelty, for all false judgments, for uncharitable thoughts toward our neighbors, and for our prejudice and contempt toward those who differ from us ..."

The litany continued, but by now I was a goner. The words had hit their mark, for they seemed to describe me perfectly even though I was now trying to be a better person. Tears were rolling out of my eyes and my heart felt like it weighed a ton. The ashes applied to my forehead seemed appropriate, for I had a genuine need to seek forgiveness.

There were weekly soup suppers on Wednesday nights during Lent at St. Christopher's and I was attending there on Sunday mornings and Tuesday evenings, too. On Thursdays it was the healing service at Grace Church. But still, I wanted more. So on Monday evenings I went to Mass at St. Edmund's Catholic church, just a block away from my apartment. The service was familiar, being very much like the Episcopal liturgy, but yet it was different and I felt like a bit of an alien.

In Holy Week, there were services at St. Christopher's every night, which I attended. It was announced that there was a sign-up sheet for the Maundy Thursday vigil, and in my ignorance I had to ask what that vigil was. The idea was that someone would be in the chapel praying constantly from

8 pm to midnight, which was based on Jesus's praying in the Garden of Gethsemene on the night when he was taken by the Roman soldiers. The three disciples who had gone there with him had fallen asleep and he asked, "Couldn't you watch with me for even an hour?" I was at St. Christopher's to do all I could do and to learn all I could, so I signed up for one of the half-hour shifts, from 9:00 to 9:30.

But then, a day or two before the vigil, one of the scripture readings was Romans 12.1, "present your bodies as a living sacrifice holy and acceptable to God." A direction was suddenly planted in my head: I should pray in the chapel for the entire four hours, not just thirty minutes, as preposterous as that sounded. I had difficulty kneeling for just a minute or two during the regular services. How could I manage it for four hours? Of course I did not have to kneel the entire time, but still, four hours sounded intimidating. It would be painful but I felt that I should try it.

Naturally I told no one of my plan, for I wasn't at all confident that physically I could carry it out. Maundy Thursday came on March 23. At the conclusion of the service, the altar was stripped of all ornaments -- the altar cloth, candlesticks, flowers, everything. And all the crosses, crucifixes and statues were draped in purple cloth. The lights were lowered, everyone filtered out of the church in silence. It was very impressive and truly mournful. The silence seemed to engulf me.

A few people went in to the chapel to pray for a while and I trailed in as well, found a comfortable pew, knelt down and began to pray. There were perhaps six of us in the small chapel. As I wrote in my journal on the next day: *I stayed for all of the vigil and spent the four hours on my knees. I* wasn't sure that I could do it or keep my mind focused on what I was there for. I wanted to confront myself with a challenge and see if I could actually meet it. I prayed the Jesus Prayer about one full hour. Then I made personal prayers and then began to read through the Psalter. At 9:30, when my time began, I moved back to prayers. Then back to Psalter (I got to Psalm 89) and then prayers till midnight.

It was at about 11:30 that something happened. Suddenly insight came flooding into my mind. I now saw a part of my life in a new light. For years I had several boxes of things from my youth, things like my scrapbooks from junior high and high school, craft projects from a summer camp I had once attended, notebooks from some of my high school classes. These things had once been very important to me because my family moved so often and we constantly had to go through our possessions and throw out all that was not essential so it would not have to be moved. By the time that I graduated from high school, our family of the peripatetic pharmacist had lived in eleven different towns in fifteen different houses and I had attended ten different schools, so we had gone through the purging of belongings fairly frequently. I had held on to these relics of my past as cherished reminders of the life that I was abandoning when we moved. *Suddenly I began to feel burdened by it all. It was so useless. It was truly a burden and I no longer wanted it. I was making relics out of my past, despising it yet unable to let go. That is so much what my life has been like. When I left the Maundy Thursday vigil, I felt differently about it. It was the dead past and I no longer needed it. It has been wonderful. I feel as if a new phase of my life has begun.*

All of this truly is what I had dreamed of. It is almost impossible to believe that it has come about. I do believe in miracles now, but this is strange and wonderful. It is hard to believe how peaceful and good my life feels now. I am amazed at how one event can transform my life. Of course I have tried to respond to that one event.

As I rose to leave the vigil at midnight, I noticed that the limp in my left foot was less severe than when I had arrived. I went home feeling cleansed and very light in spirit. The next day, Good Friday, I went to work shedding the burden of my past life. I went through my boxes and threw out almost everything. (During the Maundy Thursday vigil at St. Christopher's the following year I repeated the four-hour prayer-meditation session and again was flooded with insight and revelations. Over the years I have had people tell me that they would dearly love to have a mystical experience. I advise them to try getting down on their knees and prayer for four straight hours. Very few have been willing to do it but those few have told me that they have experienced profound and even life-changing insights.)

During the winter I began to make new friends at St. Christopher's. The most important one was Janet Jordan. She was one of the chalice bearers and when it was her turn on rotation she led the congregational prayers. She seemed very serious about her church life, was one of the leaders of the parish, and was very friendly and welcoming. In time we became friends and often we would sit by each other in church. She began to notice how cold my hands got during the services, as if I had no circulation in them at all, which was fairly close to being true. Sometimes after the services she would hold my hands in hers to warm them up. I was really amazed at how quickly she could warm them up and I began to suspect that she had some special powers. As we got to know each other, I told her of what had happened to me in England the previous summer and I mentioned my physical problems that remained. Of course my limp and difficulty in rising from the altar rail made my condition fairly obvious, but I also told her how much pain I had in my thigh, legs and feet. She then surprised me by asking, "Why are you hanging on to your pain?"

I was stunned. What could she mean? I wasn't hanging on to the pain, it was a very real condition left over from something that very nearly killed me. And then it struck me, I *was* welcoming the pain for it was because I was so very afraid that I would not re-form my life, that I would go back to the old life that I had lived in the past. The pain was my constant reminder of all that had happened to me, insuring that I did not forget. So, I guess I *was* hanging on to it.

I decided that I would buy a cross to hang around my neck. If it were always hanging there, perhaps it would remind of what I had to keep in mind and I would not have to hang on to the pain to serve that purpose. I had never worn a necklace or anything like that before but perhaps this would be good enough of a reason to change. I went to a religious bookstore and glanced through its selection of crosses. At last I found a plain and simple one, relatively small and thin. This one would do.

After several months at St. Christopher's, as much as I liked Bill and as much as I had learned from him, I began to find his constant presence oppressive. I wanted to get to know other people, too, to sit by them at times or, at other times, simply to be alone. In March I had a talk with the priest and he suggested that I try to break out on my own, to sit elsewhere if that was what I felt I needed. On the next Sunday, instead of sitting towards the front as I usually did, I sat towards the back. The service started and Bill was not there. After about ten minutes, Bill came in, found me, and sat down beside me. He seemed weak and looked terrible, pale and drawn, and he hadn't shaved that morning.

That week, on Wednesday, I was to leave for England to give my paper at the conference in Sheffield. I went to the Tuesday night healing service in the chapel as I had been doing for a couple of months. Two of the good friends that I had made at the church, Mary and Joe Monti, were there that night and we were in the parish hall talking before the service. The priest came and asked to speak with me. He told me that Bill had died, apparently from alcoholism. I was stunned and speechless almost unable to comprehend.

The service was quickly changed that night, from the regular Eucharistic prayer to a requiem service. As we moved into the prayers, tears began flowing from my eyes. The tears wouldn't stop and I was absolutely out of control. I had not cried like this when my father died and now I was crying my eyes out for someone that I had known for only a few months. Mary Monti was comforting, putting her arm around me, hugging me. Somehow in this new life of mine my emotions were very raw and close to the surface. When I returned from England, I would be starting over again, in a sense, at St Christopher's, without Bill as my friend and tutor in Episcopal ritual.

As I left for England the day following Bill's death, I reflected on how different this departure was from the one in June of the previous year. Instead of being bitterly angry and feeling alone in the world, I had people praying for me in two different parishes, St. Christophers and Grace. I felt a part of two different communities and I also felt constantly close to God. I felt the kindness of friends at the university.

After the conference in Sheffield ended, I went to London and stopped by St. Bartholomew's Hospital, making my way to the ICU. At last I could see what the place really looked like, for my perspective had been very limited when I had been there before. The ICU was actually one large room, with curtains separating the ten or so beds arranged in two facing rows. However, just off the hallway, past the nurses' station and to the right, was a different room, holding two beds, which was used for especially serious patients. This was *my* room. I recognized the blinds over the window in the door to what had been my left and the high windows on outside wall to my right. But the room seemed so small. I remembered it being much more spacious.

Everyone seemed very glad to see me, so happy that I was walking and doing so well. Now, with my vision somewhat improved and my mind much clearer, I could see who they were, too. It was also wonderful that I could actually use my voice and speak with them all now. As I stood at the nurses' station talking with several of the nurses, I looked down the row of perhaps six or so patients in the unit. One, on the right side and in the row facing me, caught my eye. He seemed to be unconscious and he had a number of I-V lines going in each arm and leg. I asked the nurses, "Is that what I looked like? Yes," one of them said, "that's exactly how you were." It shocked me, for in that state he looked so very, very ill. Nine months earlier, that had been me. It had been quite a journey since last June.

I met with a group of the physicians who had worked on me and they began asking me about my impressions of my illness and treatment, stressing how valuable it would be for them to know. One of them asked me what was the significance to me of my illness and paralysis. Uppermost in my mind was the transformation in my life that had resulted from the whole experience and I answered, "It is the greatest thing that has ever happened to me and I wouldn't give it up for all the world." They all stared at me in incomprehension.

Dr. Hinds in particular wanted to know my view of the treatment, based on the certainty that I would die, and he asked me to dictate my thoughts into his pocket recorder. I did tell him of the confusion I felt because of the constantly rotating personnel I had to face and how important it had been to me to have Sally there as something of a constant in that disorienting haze. I added that it had also been significant that she was so pretty, for it led me to want to hold on to that reality among the many others that presented themselves to me and to be at my best for her as well. "All ICU nurses should be very pretty," I added. He laughed and teased me, "I didnt know that you were such a randy chap."

While I was talking with a group of them, into the room walked the physician from my nightmare, the one who I thought had been jabbing some paralyzing agent into my arm, the one who had repeatedly forced me to inhale that awful tag. It was as if a really horrible dream had suddenly taken on tangible form and stalked into my consciousness. I stood there in complete disbelief and blurted out, "I thought you were an hallucination," which I think rather amused him.

I discovered his name was Julian Campbell and I told him of the scenes that I had experienced with him. He told me that he had not injected anything into my arm but the "hallucination" of his forcing me to inhale the tag had in fact happened. They had needed to take x-rays of my fragile lungs and it was necessary to get the tag into the proper position in one of my lungs so that it would show up on the x-ray. They had difficulties in getting it placed properly so they had indeed repeatedly pulled it back out of my lungs and had me inhale it again and again. In one way I was relieved that I hadn't hallucinated such an event, but also I was left pondering the fact that, after my experience of the Hyper-Reality of the Beyond, there was no qualitative difference between what we call "real life" and the hallucinations, there was nothing about the experience that clearly separated them, for they all had the same dreamlike quality to them.

While in London I was also able to see Sally for a short time while she took a break from work at her new hospital, and she looked so impressive wearing the blue uniform of a ward sister. The last time I had seen her my mind was still so very hazy and my eyes were very bad as well, so it was a pleasure for me to see her under these better conditions. As we were chatting, I mentioned something about the hotel in London where I was staying. She was appalled that I was having to pay outrageous sums of money there and said that the next time I was in London I should stay at her flat. In fact I did return to England in the spring of the following year (1990) and took her up on her generous offer. She was working during that time, but we did have a number of delightful conversations and she was gracious in introducing me to a number of her friends. After that we exchanged a few letters but then communication from her stopped. Perhaps she moved or married.

I also visited Sophie. I spent a few very pleasant days in Bath, spending time with her as well as seeing one of the loveliest cities in England and, along with her sister Courtney we went to the nearby ruins of Glastonbury abbey as well as Stonehenge and the Avebury ring of stones. We also had a conversation about our relationship. She explained that she had her university studies to complete, that her future was in England and that it is very difficult to sustain a long-distance relationship that stretches from Bath to Chicago. Of course all of this was true, but it was also evident that she had a romantic interest there. Within a year she was married and when I returned to England for another conference in 1990 I journeyed back to Bath and spent a few days with her and her husband.

Of course it was a disappointment that my strong feelings for Sophie and Sally, born out of the special circumstances of my illness and paralysis in London, could not be continued, but I was very heartened by a conversation I had with Fr. Trenton Pitcher, one of the Episcopal priests at Bishop Anderson House, associated with Rush-Presbyterian Hospital, whom I had met there after my repatriation from London. I felt a special attachment to him because he had seen me immediately after my return, when I was still partly paralyzed and in a very weak condition. I felt that he understood better than anyone in Chicago what had happened to me. Moreover, he is a very caring priest. A few months after my release from the hospital I went to speak with him about my great emotional attachment not only to Sally and Sophie but also to so many of the nurses and doctors at St. Bartholomew's, which at times would bring tears to my eyes when I recalled all that had happened in London.

Father Pitcher glanced away for a few seconds before he spoke. He then looked back at me and said softly, "Sometimes we have appointments in our lives, and when the appointments are met, we move on with our lives, on to other appointments." Those few words gave me great comfort and a very useful way to consider the role that all of the people at Barts had played in my life. We had our appointment as they saved my life and gave me essential encouragement and support. I could be grateful to them all and also let them go as we all moved on with our lives, on to new appointments.

In June of 1989, almost exactly a year after the beginning of illness, I was confirmed in the Episcopal Church by Frank Griswold, then bishop of Chicago and later Presiding Bishop of the Episcopal Church USA, in the cathedral of St. James, symbolically ending my apprenticeship as an Episcopalian. The significance of the event moved me very deeply and I couldn't keep my mind off a vivid remembrance of all that had happened over the past year and especially the Beyond and my paralysis and recovery. While in that state I noticed the last person to be confirmed among the hundreds present. She was a young girl, perhaps in her early teens, who was in a wheel chair and seemed to have a severe disability, perhaps cerebral palsy. She had to struggle to raise up her head and torso and to keep them up upright. After perhaps five seconds she would lose control and her body would sink down on the tray of the wheelchair. She would then struggle to raise herself up again. Flashing into my mind was the clear memory of when I was exactly like that at St. Bartholomew's, struggling even to hold my head upright, and I could feel again what my body was like then and my effort to make my muscles work and support their own weight. I was overcome by that memory and lost all composure, crying through the remainder of the service. I felt that the girl and others like her who have to make that constant struggle are the bravest people on earth.

I also had an occasion to reflect on the different path my life was on when I went back to Texas and Oklahoma to visit relatives that summer of 89. I was talking with my brother's wife and I mentioned that I was now going to church. "You!," she exclaimed with surprise, as her eyes widened, and then she broke out into wild laughter that I thought would never end. She had heard so many of my previous rantings against churches and organized religion that it seemed impossible that I could actually be in a church, much less be active in one.

* * *

By now my physical recovery was progressing very well. There were times during the past year when I would feel that I was not improving at all, for there were good days as well as bad days. On the bad days I would be exhausted and in great pain from the moment I woke up in the morning and it seemed to take all my energy to accomplish even the simplest tasks. On those days, my body would still feel as though it had been run over by a truck. But on the good days I would feel stronger and the pain would have less intensity. My improvement was so slow and incremental that I would sometimes feel that I was making no progress at all until I remembered back to my condition immediately upon leaving the hospital. In time I could twist the top off the top of cartons of milk with just my hands, I could walk greater and greater distances, and the doors at the university ceased being such a challenge for me. Except for my limp resulting from my weak left foot, one would have no idea that anything had happened to me.

Throughout the first two years of my recovery, I had one overriding concern. I knew that I was supposed to be dead but somehow divine grace and mercy had given me another chance at life. I felt that I had some specific purpose in life, but I had no idea of what it was. I wanted to know what that purpose was so that I could cooperate with it, just as I had cooperated with the divine energy when I was a quadriplegic at St. Bartholomew's. It wasn't mere idle curiosity, for it was discovering my whole reason for existence and cooperating with it. And I wanted to know immediately what it was immediately so that I could get to it. The longer I went without discovering my purpose and beginning to get to work on it seemed to indicate that I was wasting my special gift of another life. I wrote, "*I have the strongest feeling that there really is some purpose to my life now, only I don't know what it is yet, but I will try to follow where I am led,*" and I began to be attentive to a sign, any sign at all, that might lead me to that purpose.

In that first year several people either asked me if I was going to become a priest or suggested that I do so and I began to think that perhaps this was my prophetic sign. But I had two children and I had made my decision that I wanted to come back to life so that I could be around to help them, so going off to seminary seemed to be out of the question. Moreover, I felt that I was a person in progress and certainly not in an emotional state to take on the tremendous responsibilities of the priesthood. The priesthood was out but nothing was in, and my frustration and sense of failure at not finding my purpose continued to gnaw away inside me.

I had adopted the custom of going to St. Christopher"s when it was empty so that I could meditate and pray. The atmosphere was perfect for this, dark and very quiet, with the large wooden rood, the carved figure of Jesus on the cross, hanging down in the middle of the church. In this place I seemed to be able to enter a meditative state more easily. And then, one day while I was there meditating and the shimmerings began again, as I seemed to be slipping into another dimension. A vision began in my head—not the kind of vision one has with one's eyes but rather a number of vivid scenes began to play out in my head. I saw Moses on Mount Sinai wanting to see God but being told that no one can see God and live, and having to take himself into the crevice of a rock and being able to see only the back side of God as he passed by. The knowledge came to my head that often Jews will not even say the word "God" for fear of blasphemy. And then I saw Origen, the third-century Christian mystic and theologian. I can't say why I knew it was Origen, I just did —that's the way these things happen. Origen looked deeply into my eyes and said, "Now you understand, don't you? And I did, for the meaning of these pieces together made perfect sense although perhaps only to me.

It meant that we can never know God fully, for we can only know pieces of God, we can only see parts of

God. With this limitation we should never think that we can discern the mind of God or the will of God, for they are far vaster than anything that we can even imagine. Origen taught the apophatic approach to the knowledge of God, that is, knowing God through denials rather than assertions —God is not this, not that—for affirmations of God are only partial truths and can never make up the whole picture. So, the meaning was that I should not think that God's intention for me, my purpose, is in my hand, for me to figure out and complete. God can run the universe without my assistance. I should just live my life and, in living, my purpose would be fulfilled. I could relax. It made me think of the lines from *Desiderata*, the essay by Max Ehrmann, "And whether or not it is clear to you, no doubt the universe is unfolding as it should. Therefore be at peace with God, whatever you conceive him to be." I felt I could be at peace on this matter now, but I also bought a copy of Ehrmann's essay and hung it up in my apartment for those times in the future, certain to come, when I would need reminding of that basic truth.

During this time insights into the nature of God continued to flow into me. We can't know God in the normal sense because God is too transcendent to be comprehended by our puny earth-based minds, which can only comprehend other physical things on this earth. But knowing God or the nature of God is unimportant to our existence, which is really about how we live.

From my journal in March of 1990: 3/2/90: *Thoughts on God that came to me while attempting to meditate tonight: our search for God always fails while we are looking for something external, some outside, external entity, something "out there." I looked around, and God was everywhere. There was no place where God was not. God was in everything around me, was everything around me—the floors, the walls, the chair, the candle. God was in me and was me and everyone else. All of me was God. I am never away from God, never apart from God. God is all that is. It is our rational mind that attempts to grasp God and fails, for the mind cannot comprehend itself, the hand cannot grasp itself. God is truly the maker of all that is, seen and unseen, for God is all that is, seen and unseen. And God is so far beyond our comprehension that all we can produce is weak and ineffective metaphors to describe what we cannot know.*

And three months later: *God truly is in all. We can never be without God because he surrounds us at all times. To be yearning for God to be with us is like the man standing in water up to his chin and crying out for water to ease his thirst. We are always totally surrounded, submerged and subsumed by God. If we want God to be with us, we have only to look around, to open our eyes. Open our ears. Open our minds.*

The remaking of my life continued on in those first few years. Simply having a near death experience, with all of its insights and transformative aspects, does not mean that life is easy afterwards. In some ways, it is limiting and frustrating because it makes certain "normal" actions impossible. The revelations that I had received in the Beyond had given me insight into the dynamics of the relationships of my own family and I now understood our unhealthy ways of dealing with each other. I knew that I could no longer participate in them or cooperate with them, which meant that I caused trouble. I had changed, but my family had not.

While I was England the year after my illness, I discovered that, not for the first time in my life, my brother had helped himself to some of my money, in fact all of it, and had lied to me about it.

One of the issues was his use of my credit card. As we were about to land at O'Hare airport in my repatriation, Keith told me that he had used my Mastercard to pay for part of his hotel bill in London, and that I had insisted that he do so. This was news to me and I didn't think that it was true, but with my wretched memory I couldn't be certain so I said nothing.

When I went to England in 1989, I made two stays in London, one at each end of the itinerary, and I decided to stay at the same hotel where Keith had been during his six-week stay the previous year, for I knew about it and it was very close to Barts which I was going to visit. When I checked in I met the manager, Isabel Paton, whom I recognized from Keith's description of her. However I said nothing about Keith. As I was leaving for Sheffield after several days in London I brought out my Mastercard to pay my bill. Isabel began to make out the credit card form and then she paused. Looking at the card she said, "You know, there was an American staying here this past summer who had a card like this. His brother was very, very ill and in hospital here at Barts. This card reminds me of him." "I know," I responded, "I am the brother."

Isabel looked at me in disbelief and then rushed for me and gave me a giant hug. We sat down and had a nice long chat as she told me all about Keith, who had made a great impression on her. Apparently Keith had found many ways of passing the time in London and not all of his grumpy, bleary-eyed arrivals at Barts were due to poor sleep as he claimed. According to Isabel, Keith had introduced the people at the hotel in the joys of tequila in the form of his own margarita mixture and the libations had been a nightly fixture. She had been so fond of him that she had done his laundry for him during his long stay in London.

She then began talking about the credit card. "I remember him using this card to pay for his bill," she said, "and oh how he worried about what you were going to say when you found out about it." Aha, proof that I had not insisted on his using my card. It was the latest in a long series of Keith's getting money out of me by deception. In the past I would have been too afraid of Keith to confront him over the issue, but after the revelations about the family dynamics that I had received while in the Beyond, I could no longer accept this in silence.

When I returned home I called Keith and for the first time in my life, I spoke up and challenged him on the matter. I didn't say much to him, I just stated simply, "I know now that you lied to me about the card and I don't like it." I felt that it was important in putting our relationship on an honest and equitable basis. I wanted him to admit what he had done—the lying not the taking—and to apologize for the lie. I utterly failed to gain my objectives, except for my simply being able to be who I really was, and for a year he refused to speak to me. No doubt he was convinced that I was a terrible person to make an issue of what he did while being in London and looking after me. And then suddenly he began communicating again and our relationship resumed although now on a different and, at least in my eyes, healthier basis.

I also greatly distressed my mother by being honest with her about my new religious life in the Episcopal Church. For those in the Church of Christ, in which I was raised, there is only one genuine Christian church, their own, and all others are at best only paths to damnation. Thus she did not take my news well and a very unpleasant scene followed. No doubt both Keith and my mother thought I was an ingrate for being so difficult after all they had done for me during my illness and indeed they were unable to appreciate my inability to play my normal role in our traditional family games any more. I am certain that they did not think that my new life was a better one.

Back in the world, I found that I seemed to have changed in many and unexpected ways. I found that I was much more squeamish that I had been before. I could no longer watch violent movies that depict truly terrible scenes without caring about their awfulness. I walked out of *Dangerous Liaisons*, being unable to watch a movie about nothing other than people being cruel to each other. I almost left the James Bond film *License to Kill* because of its gory violence, but the episodes were few and brief and, by closing my eyes, I got by. Later I also walked out of *Pulp Fiction*, which seemed to be disgusting in every respect. Things like this had never bothered me before because I could always distance myself from the scenes. Now, however, I could not. I felt that life is so precious and is such a gift, so why would I want to spend it in watching terrible things happening, even if only on the screen? I seemed not to understand my own society and culture that could produce such movies and have them be successful.

I also didn't like walking on grass anymore, for it

didn't seem fair to the grass. I am not a fanatic about it and I am able to walk across grass if I really need to, but I prefer not to do it if possible. I also don't like killing insects and spiders if I can help it. When I find them in the house, if I can, I capture them and then release them outside where they have another chance at being what they are supposed to be.

My daughter Nissa told me that I was very much different after my illness. "You are so much calmer now, more patient, even serene," she said. My friends in Tennessee, Paul and Mary Lee, said much the same thing about two years after my illness when I was visiting them in Knoxville. They said that before my illness, when I was in the midst of my black mood, I seemed to have anger and resentment pent up inside of me. But now, they said, it seemed to be gone and instead I was at ease with the world.

However, in general I felt isolated in the world, set apart from everyone else, in sense lonely, because of what I had experienced. I felt so alone because of my insights, as if I really didn't belong in the world. It was almost as if I were straddling two very different worlds, not really in either one. Not a day goes by without my thinking of my experience and trying to incorporate its lessons into my life. In a sense, an experience of the Beyond is not confined to the time in which it is happening but rather it continues on, day after day, as a living, present reality, and I often felt that the greatest ordeal I had was to maintain my life in this world, existing as a part of it and yet at the same time being apart from it.

One source of comfort in knowing that I was not alone was my study of mysticism, which began almost immediately after I was discharged from Rush-Presbyterian.

I was still almost completely ignorant of mysticism when, a few months after my illness, I was looking over the shelves of a used book store near my apartment and saw the *Revelations* of Julian of Norwich (whom I still believed to be a man). As I was looking at the spine of the book, a voice came into my head and said "Read this." After all that had happened to me, I didn't argue, knowing that I *had* to read it although I couldn't imagine why. The *Revelations* are a marvelous introduction to mystical works, for Julian's teachings are warm, positive and engaging. Moreover, her revelations came in the course of a severe illness during which she became partially paralyzed and all those around her thought she was going to die and, for a while, she was paralyzed. Rather naturally I identified with her because of my own experiences. Oddly though, my identification with her own experiences led me to a momentary crisis. I had been seeing my own experiences as absolutely mine, unique in the world, and now I saw them as fitting into a type, a genre, and at first I was disappointed and even dejected. But then I realized that this type of experience was a marvelous one and that I was not alone in the world with my experiences, that thousands of other people in every culture had similar experiences.

Very much like the people who experienced the UFOs in *Close Encounters of the Third Kind* and then found themselves drawing countless impressions of what turned out to be Devil's Tower without understanding why they were doing it, I was driven by some force to read about mysticism. I bought everything on mysticism at the nearby used book store and then went on to a different one in town and began buying everything there on the subject there as well. Again my world was shaken by reading the accounts of mystical experiences, for they seemed so much like my own, both that of the Beyond and afterwards. The exposure to mysticism caused me to reflect on the meaning of my experiences: *I have been so bothered by my revelations. They sound so similar to conditions and substance to so many others—is this some by-product of illness, a kind of hallucination? Now I think I had the experience because I was so nearly dead. I managed to get free of myself and become aware, aware of God. That is why severe illnesses produce these experiences. It is also why it doesn't fade away with time and with recovery, why near-death experiences are so life-transforming. They are glimpses into Reality.*

After about a year of this intense reading, I wanted to understand mysticism in a more systematic fashion and I decided that the best way to gain this was to teach it, which would force me to focus my reading and sharpen my knowledge, so I signed myself up to teach an upper-level course on medieval mysticism. The principal focus was on medieval mystics, but we also ranged widely on the general topic, discussing Buddhism, Judaism, Islam and even Native American religion. As the course progressed, there was much discussion of many of the various aspects of mysticism, and my own views on mysticism began to deepen, often on the basis of my own experiences: *Revelation by end of mysticism class today: I am not interested in the uniate stage of mysticism, but only in the experiential aspects. Seeking union implies purpose and a system that one can affirm. I distrust overt purpose, for the end could be self-induced. I can't support an intricate system. I simply want to live my life in concord with what I experienced, to be prepared for my next death, to trust in God and walk with God. I want only to enjoy the now, truly and simply. I don't want to be dissatisfied with now because of what it isn't. I want to see God all around me and not assume that God is elsewhere. I don't want to construct my idol of God or of religion, which I will then worship. I believe that here and now and ordinary life are good enough. None of it matters anyway. There is not an obvious advantage to the mystical path or union or any of the rest of it. I feel the Buddhist in me is coming out very strongly—no big deal, purposelessness, non-grasping.*

And shortly later, I wrote: *I am still having strong reaction against mystical systems and especially against the idea of union. I do not at all doubt the validity of my experience, which I do consider mystical, nor do I doubt the continuing revelations. I can't possibly doubt the improvement in my life. What I am increasingly struck by is the unknowability of God, the transcendence of the immanent God. I am coming ever more to believe that we should keep silence before God, and about God as well. ... Union seems far off, and it seems like grasping, trying to force things to be a certain way, desiring; it smacks of system. I think just sitting and waiting is the best thing -- union will come or it won't, but really it doesn't matter. I think, in a Zen way, there already is union and all that we can do is to recognize it. Isn't that what meditation will do? It will help diminish the interference and static that interferes with this communication and awareness. Perhaps a mystical life is just waking up, not trying to make something happen. Mysticism is awareness of what is. No big deal. It is Zen. It is Tao. It is Christianity. It is.*

There is no attainment of union, only awareness of union.
It is difficult to accustom our awareness to this fact -- that
is, the mystic way, the long struggle to keep this awareness.

As I taught the course that term and in the following years, I found the existing books on mysticism to have largely missed the things that to me are the central point of mysticism, that is, the mystical experiences themselves and the effects they had on the lives of the mystics. Scholars who study mysticism seem to be fascinated with the thought of mystics—almost an oxymoronic concept—and rather embarrassed about their subjects' actual mystical experiences. It was this dissatisfaction with the existing books on mysticism that led me eventually to write my own book, *Mystics of the Christian Tradition*, which emphasizes the mystical experiences themselves and their transformative effects on the lives of the mystics I discussed.

My sense of isolation also began to ebb when I discovered Near Death Experiences. Two years after my illness I was on a committee at the university and got to know another member of the committee, Neal Grossman, a member of the Philosophy Department. Our friendship began when we discovered that we both taught courses on mysticism in our own departments, and Neal also taught on the philosophy of religion and on death and dying as well. Neal and I were serving on a subcommittee and he came by my office so that we could get about our assignment when I saw that he was carrying a copy of Raymond Moody's *Life After Death*. I asked him what that book was for. Somewhat awkwardly, wary that I might scorn him, he told me that he was teaching on the Near Death Experience and he was looking for someone who had had one. Suddenly I had a new label for what I had experienced in the Beyond and I said, "I've had one."

Neal was delighted and asked me to tell him about it, which I did. He then asked me if I would talk to his class about my experience because he thought it would mean so much more to them if they heard it from a real person than if they simply read about such experiences in their book. I was very hesitant, for I had told only a handful of people about my experience and now to do so to a large room of total strangers would be very difficult, but in the end I agreed. I believed that perhaps it was my duty to tell others about that experience, to give others an opportunity to learn what I had learned. Despite being very nervous and self-conscious, I told his class my story and did my best to answer their questions.

The following term Neal asked me to speak to his new classes, which I did, and then again the next term as well. Finally I had to refuse. I feared that my presentation was beginning to become formulaic and "canned." Simply pull the string and out comes my story, devoid of the feelings and emotions attached to it. But I didn't want that to happen, for this was the most important and precious thing that ever happened to me and I didn't want its significance to wane or to become watered down for me.

Now, however, I became aware of a large body of literature on NDEs, into which I threw myself with a passion. It was fascinating for me to read about other people's experiences, some very similar to my own. However, I kept being bothered by the fact that I had not had the "tunnel experience" that was in so many of the published accounts of NDEs, especially because when I talked to Neal's classes that was the first thing they wanted to know about. In fact it seems to be the most common popular image of the Near Death Experience. I began to wonder if maybe I had experienced only a little NDE or maybe an incomplete NDE or maybe that I had simply forgotten it. It is so easy to become competitive about the quality of one's NDE. But I was comforted to a degree when I read in Raymond Moody's *The Light Beyond* that the "tunnel" experience figures in only 9% of near death experiences, and encountering other beings is in 23% of NDEs. Two of my own experiences, encountering a principal being and having the life review were among the most common, both at 32%. Then in 2002 I met Melvin Morse, the pediatrician who has done some of the principal research on NDEs, and especially in children, which he has published in such books as *Closer to the Light* and *Transformed by the Light*. In his opinion the "tunnel" only came into prominence with the appearance of Moody's *The Light Beyond*, which enshrined it in the popular imagination, and he said that he did not see it as a necessary element in the NDE.

The most similar life review to my own was in Dannion Brinkley's book *Saved by the Light*, where he described having to experience others' experience of himself, to feel the pain and grief that others felt because of his actions. He, too, wrote of the unpleasantness of this experience. I was also fascinated when he wrote that, as he left "the Crystal City" (which was not part of my experience), he faded into a rich blue-grey atmosphere, which is exactly the color of my first memory of the Beyond.

Through my reading on the Near Death Experience I felt less isolated in the world, less strange and weird with my experiences. Many NDEers come back with a profound sense of having a specific purpose in life, but one that is unknown to them, and feel a great urgency to discover that purpose to begin fulfilling it. They tend to have their lives transformed by their experiences in a dramatic and positive manner. Moreover, the general world view of NDEers is very similar to my own. But perhaps one of the most amazing finds in the NDE literature was how common it is for such people to return with increased psychic abilities and, specifically, with healing abilities. This aspect was of particular comfort for by now my own experiences with healing work had begun.

CHAPTER 7

Adventures in Healing

My initiation into an entirely different aspect of healing started without warning. It was the summer of 1991, three years after my illness, and my daughter Nissa, who was then thirteen, was having a severe headache. I gave her some acetaminophen, which didn't make a dent in the headache. Then a voice, my voice but not my voice, was in my head, telling me that I could help her. That was it, "You can help her." It didn't tell me how I should do this, but I did have a mental picture of putting my fingers up to her temples. But I rejected the voice. "This is nuts," I thought, "this is not sane." Nothing in my life had prepared me to consider "faith healing" as legitimate, and certainly this was nothing that I wanted be involved with. As a boy I had watched Oral Roberts on television, grasping the heads of the faithful and seeming to give them a good shaking. At the time, the whole scene seemed laughable.

However, my own healing from paralysis had indeed been miraculous and I didn't doubt that such miracles could happen anywhere at any time. Moreover, my recovery had happened when I cooperated with the power that I felt flowing into me. I didn't like the idea of not cooperating with the divine. But for me to help heal others? I didn't feel that I was the kind of material for doing such things but I resolved that I would not turn down another invitation to do something.

I didn't have to wait very long. About a week later, the same thing happened. My daughter got another headache and again the acetaminophin did nothing. And again, my voice which was not my voice told me, "You can help her." So I raised my hands, put my index fingers against her temples, and swiftly pulled them away after a couple of seconds. She stared at me with great surprise, eyes wide open, and said, "How did you do that? It's gone."I couldn't say anything, for I didn't know what I had done. But now I was stunned. The headache was gone. What did this mean? I was both attracted to the idea of helping others experience unexpected healing and resistant to the entire concept.

More importantly, now what? I discussed what happened with friends at church and one of them said that perhaps I had "the gift." I also discussed the matter with a friend who is very well tuned in to psychic matters and asked if she had any ideas on the subject. She related it to my experience of the Beyond and added, "You don't come back without a gift." I also read in the literature concerning Near Death Experiences that it is common for people who come back from an NDE to have increased psychic abilities, and in Margot Grey's *Return From Death*, gifts of healing are specifically mentioned as frequent byproducts of NDEs, a point that was also emphasized by Kenneth Ring in his book *Lessons From the Light*. Nonetheless, I felt very unsure about the whole matter and decided just to follow what presented itself to me, and as it turned out events seemed to push me along.

Intrigued by what my hands had been involved in, the first thing I noticed was that if I brought my palms within an inch or two of each other and then moved them around in small circles, I could feel energy around them on my palms. It was much like the feeling of bringing two magnets together and having the same poles face each other, producing a feeling of invisible tangibleness as they repel each other. I did not know what that feeling was, but I knew that it was real and the body does have something that can be called an "aura." Moreover, with two teenaged children, I had frequent opportunities to deal with headaches, growing pains and sports injuries, and I tentatively began to try to repeat what had originally happened and, amazingly, the same results were achieved. Almost always there would be an immediate and complete or almost complete healing of the pain. My son Soren had a terrible headache, and I put one hand above his forehead, the other behind his neck. When I took my hands away, he was amazed that the headache was gone and asked me how I learned to do that, and he then added, "Dad, you should write a book about that." Luckily from the beginning of this healing work I have been keeping an account of events in my journal and thus I have a relatively complete record of everything that has happened, with dates and details.

At about this same time I had come out of my self-imposed isolation and Sarah had come into my life. Once we began to date and our relationship deepened, I was provided with a new person with a variety of health problems on whom I could work as well as opportunities to explore someone else's bodily aura. Sarah had headaches, abdominal cramps, colds, as well as painful pressure from her wisdom teeth pushing against the other teeth so that at times it was very difficult for her even to open her mouth. Just as with my children, after I waved my hands over the areas or put my hands on them, almost always the pain or cramps were relieved immediately or, with the cold and sniffles, greatly improved.

During this time I discovered that, for the most part, I could only feel the body's aura when there was some problem due to pain or injury and then I could feel it quite distinctly. The "invisible tangibleness" could have a variety of shapes and textures. It could feel like a mound or ridge or even a cone, and it could feel smooth or rough or even raspy. Typically a migraine was tightly coiled around the head as if the person were wearing a cap made of steel wool. Not knowing exactly what I should be doing, I decided that I would move my hand around in the air in the aura until it felt smooth and less distinct or, on other occasions when the feeling struck me, I would just place my hand down on the skin at the spot and hold it there for a while, usually about two to five minutes. I would concentrate on sending healing energy into the area and then on pulling out the pain. I also noticed that very frequently when my hand would move over such an area of disrupted aura, my face would start tingling with a very strong "creepy-crawly" feeling running over it, so strong that often I would have to stop and scratch my face. I decided to take that feeling as a sign that I should stop and work on that spot. On the negative side, often after I would do this work I would feel sharp pain in my hands and frequently I would feel nauseous although, thankfully, the feeling would usually pass after I would lie down for a few minutes. After several years I learned that if I would symbolically wipe the pain off my hands after I worked on someone, these side effects could be avoided, while another effective technique was to visualize the pain and discomfort flowing through my body and down through my feet into the earth.

The people on whom I work tell me that they feel a variety of sensations. Sometimes they feel that "invisible tangibleness," the magnetic sensation that I also feel, but sometimes they feel heat or even electrical, "sparking" sensations. Sometimes the pain worsens while I am actually moving my hands over them. It is impossible to predict when the improvement in their condition will come. It might be immediately, or perhaps a few hours later or even the next day. Especially when I am working on someone's head, they might also see colors, with white and purple being the most common.

Sarah and I also discovered a playful side to the healing work. I had my hand on Sarah's stomach to try to help her with a stomach ache when she started to sneeze. Just as the sneeze was about to explode, I pulled my hand away from her stomach but the sneeze never came. She looked at me and said, "Hey, you stole my sneeze." Some months later as again she was about to sneeze, I tapped her forehead with my finger and again the sneeze was stopped in its tracks. A few days later she had the hiccups, which, with Sarah, could last for hours, so I tapped her forehead in the same spot and in the same manner as with the sneeze and instantly the hiccups ceased. Sarah gave me a strange look as though I were a freak. In these early months of experimentation,

Sarah had an incredible amount of stomach gurgling and once she playfully asked me to make it quiet. I had doubts about using the healing in this frivolous manner but she insisted. I put my hand on her stomach and the gurgling indeed ceased immediately, but then Sarah said that it felt as if her esophagus were blocked and she felt ill for the rest of the day. I offered to try to help her with her new problem but she refused, saying that it was cosmic punishment for being so stupid.

I have also done this sort of work on inanimate objects. One winter day when my friend Charles Wells was leaving my house after a treatment, he found that his car wouldn't start. He came back inside and I offered to give him a ride home but he wanted to give his car another try. We went back to his car, raised the hood and tightened all the connections we could find. Charles then tried starting it again and the car cranked away, but showed no signs of starting. Because the hood was up and Charles was behind the wheel, I thought he wouldn't see me and I reached down and touched one of the electrical parts. Immediately the car started. Charles, who had in fact seen me, got out of the car and said that I was in the wrong line of work, I should go into auto repair. Several years later, as she was returning from a business trip, Sarah's small bag containing her laptop computer fell off her larger bag onto the floor. Sarah hoped that the fall had been cushioned but two days later when she turned on her computer nothing happened at all. No lights, no noises, nothing. She plugged in the AC adaptor but found the same result. It was as if the computer had died. She asked me if I would work on the laptop but again I had reservations—we had learned not to fool around with healing, but Sarah said that she wasn't fooling around, she needed her laptop for her work. We tried booting it up again, including another try with the adaptor, but still there was absolutely nothing. I then moved my hand over the keyboard and I could feel "disruptions," which I worked at smoothing out for two or three minutes. Sarah then turned on the computer and it booted right up, to her delight and my own surprise.

I discovered a new and interesting aspect of the healing work when Sarah and I went on our honeymoon following our marriage and Sarah immediately came down with a severe cold. We were on a train in Belgium and Sarah was sleeping although still coughing incessantly. While she slept, I placed my hand above her throat and within a few minutes her coughing ceased completely. When she awoke, I asked her how her cough was and she said it was fine, it was gone. Because she had been unaware that I was trying to help heal her, the improvement could not be said to be the result of any placebo effect.

A few months after that, Sarah came home from work with another sore throat and very scratchy voice and she asked me to help her. I held my left hand over her throat for about ten minutes and when I pulled it away I noticed that my wedding ring seemed awfully tight on my finger. With some difficulty I pulled it off to look at it and, to my astonishment, it was no longer circular but had somehow been pressed into an oval that was uncomfortably tight on my finger. I took the ring off and began working on it. One after another I held sections of the ring between two fingers and tried to send energy into them. Then, after a section was "softened," I pushed on the ring to bend it back more into the proper shape. I succeeded in restoring it to a more or less circular shape, though with many irregularities, so that it was, more accurately, roughly octagonal. An odd thought crossed my mind -- here I had been worried about becoming like Oral Roberts but instead I had become like Yuri Geller!

Whenever I did this work, I felt that, without a doubt, it was something that I should be doing, that this was right for me. The problem was that I didn't have a clue as to what I should be doing, I was simply improvising everything I did. Should I hold my hand above the body or on it? Should I move my hand around or simply leave it in one spot? Was one minute sufficient, or five, or ten? Should I be sending energy in or pulling pain out, or both? Should I be thinking anything in particular? I knew no one who did anything like this and, other than watching televangelists whose genuineness I suspected, I had never seen it done.

A couple of years earlier one of my students had given me a book that he thought would be good for me, Agnes Sanford's *The Healing Light*. (Sanford was the daughter of Christian missionaries to China, the wife of an Episcopal priest, and a true mystic and healer of considerable power, as I discovered several years later when I read her fascinating autobiography, *Sealed Orders*.) When I first received the book I thanked my student politely but it held absolutely no interest to me and I filed it away in my bookcase. But now, there it was, waiting for me. I retrieved it, blew the dust off the top of the pages and read it through with keen interest. This was the beginning of my exposure to the wide, strange world of healing. I was comforted in discovering that there were people who practiced healing in simple sincerity without the excesses of the televangelists and I no longer felt alone in the world with what I was doing.

Moreover, it was wonderful to discover new concepts and techniques that I might never have developed on my own. In particular I was struck by Sanford's idea that one could heal oneself of various injuries and ailments by placing one's own hand on the affected area and saying something like, "I am a child of God, I am not intended to suffer harm." Soon I had an opportunity to put that theory in practice when, as I was ironing my shirts, I reached across the iron and accidentally touched my wrist against it. A blister appeared while redness spread over a wide area around it. Once I finished my ironing I could deal with my burn and I tried out the method described by Agnes Sanford. I put the first two fingers of my right hand on top of the blister and, despite the intense pain that it caused, I kept them there for about thirty minutes, repeating Sanford's recommended mantra. I then removed my fingers and, to my surprise, the redness was gone and where the blister had been there was now only a red streak. There was no blister, no pain. A few months later we were at Sarah's grandmother's house and as I was leaning against a kitchen counter, I moved my arm against a hot deep-fat fryer that had just been used for making french fries and again I burned my arm on it. I immediately put my index finger over the burned area, which again caused the burn to hurt far more intensely, but I kept it in place for about ten minutes. The next morning the redness was diffused over a wide area and there was no blister and no pain. This was really amazing.

I continued my reading program on healing with Francis McNutt's books *The Power to Heal* and *Healing*, which introduced me to the practices of distant healing,

healing people at some distance away simply by praying without working on them in person, and "soaking prayer," when a group of people pray together intensively for distant healing on someone. I soon had an opportunity to try these methods out when Sarah's grandmother returned from a Caribbean cruise feeling very ill, as though she had the flu. After several months passed she had not improved despite the medical treatment she was receiving. Sarah was growing very concerned for her grandmother so one night at the Thursday evening healing service at Grace Church we decided to try our version of soaking prayer on her by concentrating together intently and praying for her healing. My working on her directly was completely out of the question because she was so strongly opposed to anything that smacked of religion. To our relieved amazement, the next day Sarah's grandmother was feeling better and on the second day she was perfectly fine, just like that, after months of illness. Of course we never mentioned our prayers for her.

In the years that followed I discovered that this sort of soaking prayer for people, without actually waving my hand over them or touching them, seems to be followed by remarkable improvements involving colds, muscle pains, cases of the flu and even some who had cancer. One woman was suffering from the effects of breast cancer to such an extent that she had been forced to take a leave from her work and it was feared that she would die in a matter of days. However, after the prayers for her began she was able to go back to work and she lived two more years before she eventually died of the cancer. Of course one cannot claim that the prayers for distant healing were solely responsible for the recovery of all of these people, for other people were also praying for them and usually they were also receiving normal medical attention. Nonetheless, the recoveries were remarkable and when I do this sort of prayer for someone, I normally expect recovery or significant improvement to become noticeable within forty-eight hours.

I developed several methods of this distant healing prayer, all being forms of visualization. In one method I hold up an image of the person in my mind and, after saying a prayer for their healing, I visualize white or golden light flowing into them and I visualize their recovery, picturing them standing in perfect health. If I am asked to pray for someone unknown to me, I ask for a picture of the person, which I then use for the same sort of visualization. However, often I am not given a picture of the person to be prayed for, in which case I visualize the person who requested the prayers and then visualize a ray of connection between that person and the one to be prayed for, and then I visualize the healing flowing out from the requester into the outline of the person who is the one being prayed for. However, often I visualize myself with the person to be prayed for and, using one of these techniques, I visualize myself placing my hands on the person just as if I were with them, with healing power flowing into them and pain being removed. In time I began to move my hands in the air over the visualized image of the person and, to my surprise, in my hands I felt that same invisible tangibleness as I do when the person is actually in front of me. I don't understand it but it is there and it seems to help as I go through the visualization routine.

Over the past several years as I have given talks on mysticism and healing I have described this technique of healing prayer and it has attracted considerable attention from those who are especially interested in healing. At our church enough people were drawn to it that we have formed a small group, with a core of five or six of us, but we have had as many as twenty, who meet twice a month to use this form of prayer for parishioners and friends who have health problems. While we cant claim that people's recovery from illness or injury is due to our prayer, it does seem that when we join our visualization prayers together in this fashion good things seem to happen. When I talk on the subject I point out that I don't believe that there is any single technique that is best or more effective than another and that everyone should use the form of visualization that seems best and most natural to them.

Meanwhile, in the six months that followed the beginning of my experiences in healing, I became overwhelmed with a mixture of amazement and apprehension. My amazement came because the healings were usually complete or nearly complete and usually happened immediately or within a few hours, and there seemed to be no limit to what might be healed. I was apprehensive because it seemed as though this healing work was my destiny but I could not imagine what the consequences might be. If this were my destiny I would have to respond to it and if the healings worked on others as they did with my children and Sarah, I would be swarmed by people, just like the televangelists for whom I was gaining a degree of increased respect. In my imagination I saw a line of people waiting outside my door, all wanting healing. But still I did not know what to do next.

My own miraculous healing had been so obviously connected to the divine and I felt so clearly directed into the Episcopal Church that I believed whatever I did should be within the church. After all, most Episcopal churches seemed to have regular healing services where people receive anointings for themselves or for others for whom they prayed, so I was convinced that there was some way that this healing could be used within the church. The immediate catch was that while my own priest did offer the laying on of hands at the Tuesday evening services which I was now attending regularly, he was generally distrustful of the healing ministry and himself did not really believe in miraculous healing. He once told me that he did the laying on of hands because, in a sort of divine placebo effect, he thought that people would do better if they believed that God was with them. I did not expect my priest to be very positive when I told him of all of this weirdness, but I thought I owed it to him to give him a chance. I requested a meeting with him and then told him all that had happened.

To my surprise he didn't seem shocked by my story. I included the account of how my ring became an oval and how I had straightened it. I took off the ring and handed it to him, and he slowly inspected the ring, which he had seen in its original form when he married Sarah and me several months earlier, and noted its many current irregularities. He looked at me with a quizzical expression, "I have no experience in this area," he said, "so I really can't give you any advice. But, I tell you what, I'll discuss this with an older, more experienced priest and I'll get back to you." About a week later he finally had some word for me. "Well, I decided to take up this matter with Bishop Griswold. He is very interested in the healing ministry and he knows a Jesuit who is a healer. He will get you in touch with the

Jesuit, but meanwhile he thinks that you should not do any more healing for anyone else."

I was elated and excited for at last I could talk to someone about this and perhaps gain some direction. After about a month passed, after the Sunday service I asked my priest if he had heard anything from the bishop, did he have the name of the Jesuit? He answered, "No, I've heard nothing, but if I haven't heard anything by the end of the week, I'll give Bishop Griswold a call." After two weeks passed, I asked him the same question and received the same answer. Two weeks later we repeated the identical conversation. By now I was frustrated and a bit angry, feeling that I was not being dealt with honestly, suspicious that his distrust of healing was at work.

I decided that if there were a Jesuit healer in Chicago I could find him, after all, I was a trained professional researcher. I called the Jesuit provincial headquarters in Chicago and simply asked the receptionist if she knew of such a person. There was a long pause and, after being put on hold for a while, I was given the name of a priest at Loyola University Chicago who might be able to answer the question. I called the priest and asked him if he knew of a Jesuit who was a healer. Very quickly he said, "You must mean Father Robert Sears, who is at Jesuit House at the University of Chicago," and he gave me the phone number. I called Father Sears and made an appointment to see him.

Father Sears was tall and thin and had a friendly, thoughtful appearance. He interviewed me extensively about what I was doing and about my religious life, and finally concluded that he did not think that my healing work was coming from the dark side. It was a positive sign, he thought, that I wanted to do it in the church. He did, however, caution me of dangers in doing this work, for evil spirits react against healing, both in those being healed and those doing the healing. He said, "If you continued with this work, people would turn against you and that you could have ego problems. I advise you to remember that the object of this work is not healing but rather understanding, and you should always keep this point in your mind." He also warned me, "You cannot heal everyone, you must have limits for yourself. Some people do not want healing and others do not need healing in order to understand." Finally he also counseled me to beware of evil spirits. Father Sears concluded by giving me some of the articles on healing that he had written and stated that he wished that he could do more for me, but, he said, "You're an Episcopalian, you really should talk with the bishop of Chicago because he is very interested in healing work." I sighed and answered, "In a way, I already tried that avenue and it didn't really work out the way I wanted it to."

After I left Father Sears, I excitedly called up my own priest and asked to speak with him. After settling down in a chair beside his desk, I proudly told him, "I was able to find that Jesuit healer that the bishop mentioned and I have just talked with him." "Bob Sears?" my priest asked. I sat there stunned. I had been so anxious to find my elusive Jesuit healer and had repeatedly asked my priest if he had heard anything from the bishop, and the answer was always negative, yet here he already knew the Jesuit's name and had said nothing to me. I felt terribly let down and, no doubt unfairly, I also felt betrayed. Probably from that moment my relationship with him was doomed. Moreover, Father Sears' warnings about the problems that I would have seemed to have already been fulfilled.

About the time I began my search for Father Sears, I had talked to Bill Burks, the priest of Grace Church, the other Episcopal Church, whose Thursday evening healing services I had been attending for about five years, and asked if he could give me any direction. Bill was also baffled by my story, saying that he had never encountered anything like it before but he would do what he could. Bill called the diocesan office and within a day told me that there was no nearby branch of the Order of St. Luke, an inter-denominational organization dedicated to healing and healing prayer, but he did have the name and address of an Episcopal priest who was a healer, the Reverend Canon Mark Pearson in Pennsylvania. I immediately wrote a letter to Father Pearson, briefly explaining my situation and asking if he had any guidance that he could offer. Several months later I got a response. He sent me back my own letter with his own handwritten note in the margin, suggesting that I talk with him when he would be in Chicago holding a healing mission a few months later. That was it. As the date of the mission drew close I called up the suburban Episcopal church where Father Pearson would be and I asked if I could make an appointment to talk with him, but I was told that he had no free time during his Chicago trip because he would be going to Wrigley Field to a Cubs game. Sarah and I then attended Father Pearson's healing mission with the hope that I could talk with him there.

It was an enlightening although not entirely positive experience. Father Pearson's books were on display at the church and I bought a copy of one of them, *Christian Healing*, and settled in my seat in the packed church. Father Pearson preached a nice sermon on healing and then opened the service up for laying on of hands to all who were interested, and virtually all in attendance were interested. Lay members of that parish's Order of St. Luke were stationed around the altar area also to lay hands on people and to offer counseling. As I waited in line down the central aisle for Father Pearson's laying on of hands, a woman just ahead of me swooned at his touch, the "slaying in the spirit" that I had read about in Francis MacNutt's books, a phenomenon seen regularly in virtually all the healing services of the televangelists.

At the close of the service Father Pearson took up a position at the rear of the church to greet people as they left. When I reached him, I quickly blurted out, "I'm the person who wrote to you about healing work, you wrote me back that I should see you when you were in Chicago." He smiled and said, "Good to meet you," and shifted his eyes to greet the person in line behind me, whom he also greeted with a friendly "Good to meet you" before moving on to the next person. Dejectedly I moved on out of the church and into the dark of the night, feeling let down again as I recalled the warnings of Father Sears. This was not going to be easy.

Meanwhile Bill, the priest at Grace Church, was supportive of my involvement in healing work and was urging me to tell the group that usually attended the Thursday evening service about this healing work that had entered my life. I resisted, for I was uncomfortable about making public these very strange events in my life, but Bill persisted. "Oh come on, Steve," he said in his soft Tennessee drawl, "It'll be good for you to tell the others about all this. They all attend this healing service regularly, they already believe in healing, they'll accept it and you, too." I gave in and Bill arranged for me to give the homily at the next Thursday evening service. With my heart pounding, I stood at the lectern and disclosed to the five or six people there what I was doing and added some words about various meanings of "healing," not all of which implied instantaneous, complete physical healing. After the service, two of those in attendance, who were from Ghana, came up to me and we talked about this kind of healing in their own culture, but other than that, none of those who heard my story ever mentioned the subject to me again. After my great psychological crisis, this too was a great letdown and it began to seem that no matter what I did, nothing ever resulted. Bill soon left the parish and the only cleric who had actively tried to help me was gone from my life.

In the months that followed, I continued my reading of books about healing. Especially helpful were the books on the technique of Therapeutic Touch that I found, *The Therapeutic Touch* by Dolores Krieger and *Therapeutic Touch, A Practical Guide* by Janet Macrae. I discovered that the technique used there was basically the one that I had evolved on my own, being extremely practical but lacking any religious or spiritual basis. However, those books describe how one can feel hot and cold spots as one's hands pass above the body of the person being worked on, but I have never felt such sensations, only the invisible tangibleness and "creepy-crawlies."

Morton Kelsey's book on the history of healing within Christianity, *Psychology, Medicine & Christian Healing*, provided a useful historical background and I discovered that Kelsey, an Episcopal priest who taught at Notre Dame, had been Agnes Sanford's parish priest and recommended her book *The Healing Light*, which had led him to take seriously the healing ministry. My reading also took in books of a more decided New Age tone, such as Barbara Brennan's *Hands of Light*, which acquainted me with the theory of the body's chakras and how they could be used in healing. Larry Dossey's book *Healing Words* was also important to me for his argument for scientifically demonstrable evidence of the effectiveness of prayer in bringing about healing. I also found it interesting that Dossey recommended a generalized prayer along the lines of "thy will be done" as being the most effective, while Agnes Sanford advocated very specific prayer for someone, believing that a generalized prayer would not attain results. I found that reading widely while reserving judgment and following one's inner feelings is probably the best method in investigating healing.

The entire body of reading was very helpful in making me familiar with a variety of techniques and theories while also forcing me to think seriously about the entire subject of healing and to develop a philosophy of healing. I had to ask myself *why* I was doing this work, was physical healing really so important, and why did the healing work most times but not on other occasions?

I came to believe that on some occasions physical ailments are manifestations of psychological or spiritual problems. My introduction to the reality of that phenomenon came when I was working on a friend of mine who had severe neck pains. I worked on her several times over the space of three weeks yet she never experienced any relief from her problem. While working on her, I was surprised that I never felt any disruption of the body's aura over that area but instead it always felt perfectly normal. After considering the matter and remembering some of the books that I had read, I asked her who was the pain in the neck in her life. She immediately answered that it was her husband, who was not employed and seemed to be chasing one wild scheme after another without accomplishing anything. All of the burden of supporting them was falling on her. She said that she had been meaning to have a serious talk with him about the problem and she was hoping to set some deadline after which, if none of his schemes panned out he would get a regular job. When we parted, she said that she was going to have the talk with him that night. The next day she called me up and said, "Well, you healed my neck," explaining that indeed that night they had discussed the whole matter and had reached the agreement that she hoped for. When she woke up the next morning, the pain in her neck was entirely gone.

About a year later I was working on a man who had back pains and again my work on him did nothing to help him and I could feel no disruption around his back. Applying the lesson I had learned earlier, I asked, "who is the pain in the back in your life?" It turned out that it was his girlfriend, with whom he had been wanting to break up but so far had not been able to summon the courage actually to do it. When the relationship finally ended, so did the pains in his back. In these two cases I could have spent hours waving my hands over their painful areas and nothing would ever have been accomplished because the underlying cause, which was not physical at all, remained unchanged. Thus I learned that there are times when we should think symbolically about our illnesses and pains.

I also came to understand that healing is not a clearly defined concept. In my own case, my illness in London and the resulting paralysis had brought about spiritual and psychological healing that transformed my life. For me, the illness itself brought about healing and I would not want to have been spared those physical problems. A few months after I was released from the hospital I read an account of a woman who had been aboard an Egyptian airliner that had been hijacked by terrorists. As an American she was taken to the door of the plane, shot in the head and thrown down to the airport tarmac. She survived the attempt to kill her although she suffered some mental problems and many physical limitations as a result of the damage done to her brain, yet she said it was the best thing that had ever happened to her and she was glad that it had happened. A suspicion entered my mind that perhaps she had similar experience to mine and valued the changes that it had brought to her life.

About ten months after the healing work began in my life, my mother died of pancreatic cancer. She had never been the most psychologically stable person and I was fearful that she would panic as her death neared. But when I was visiting her about six weeks before she died, I was amazed at the calmness she displayed, because for the first time that I had ever seen, she was at peace internally. She seemed wise, even noble, and I thought that it was because of her illness. Somehow it seemed as though this is how a person should be when facing death.

I also remembered the story told by my friend Bill, the priest. As best I remember it, he said that, after leaving seminary he was at his first parish, in the mountains of east Tennessee. He was called out to visit an ailing parishioner who had a much younger wife who eyed him suspiciously as he entered their cabin. Bill asked her, "What to you want me to do?" She replied, "You're a priest aren't you, heal him." Very nervously Bill began the healing rite and started to anoint the old man, who promptly died as Bill's hands were on him. "He croaked on me, the old man croaked on me," Bill told me. Bill then looked up at the man's wife, worrying how she would react. "Thank you," she said, "he's healed now." Sometimes death itself is a healing.

In looking at the question of healing in a larger perspective, I came to believe that it is not physical healing that is most important, but rather spiritual and psychological healing. Therefore perhaps the principal reason that I wanted to do healing was to show that there is something beyond the merely physical that is a reality in our lives, and my own recovery from paralysis stands as another example of this same fact although I also am pleased that I can offer to people the possibility of relief from illness and pain.

Over the next few years I struggled to learn to distance myself from the results of what I was doing. If there was a cure, it was not because of me, for I only served as a conduit for the healing power, and if there was no observable cure, it was not because I had done something wrong nor did it negate the healings that did take place. Being able to take the results in stride and, in a sense, without getting attached to results, was one of the most important and most difficult lessons that I had to learn. I simply continued on as I had before, doing healing work when an opportunity presented itself, mostly with Sarah and my daughter, and with a few friends to whom I slowly opened up and offered to try to help them. When I saw them in pain I felt badly if I did absolutely nothing, so I would say tentatively, "I don't know if I can do anything or not, but I might be able to help you." I then would explain the technique, pointing out that I wouldn't even touch them. In time I came to trust my hands, confident that what I was feeling was genuinely the body's aura disrupted by injury or illness. One of my friends was having some serious problems in her back and as I worked on her I felt a very definite area of disruption at the top of her lumbar region and I pointed it out to her. However, she kept insisting that her back hurt in a different spot. Then one day when she saw me she laughed and told me that she had just gone to her doctor for an injection in her back to try to help her with her back pain, and the spot where the injection was given, the place of the damaged disk, was exactly where I had been saying that I had been feeling the disruption all along. As is often the case with nerve damage, the damage can easily be in one place and the pain displaced to another. As incidents like this multiplied, I came to rely on my hands to tell me where problems were and to trust that the information was correct, which I feel is essential in doing healing work.

Not all of my efforts to heal other people have met with success, however. I worked on one man with chronic, severe migraines and he continued to have those attacks after I worked on him. Unfortunately he never had a migraine when he came to see me and the treatments could not serve as migraine prophylactics even though I had worked on a number of people who were having migraines at the time and they always had their migraines cease after I worked on them. After about six sessions, he finally decided that he was going to get no relief from my efforts and our meetings stopped.

My greatest frustration during the first two years was that nothing much seemed to be happening with the healing work that initially I feared would take over my life. As I wrote of concerns in my journal: *Perhaps I ought not to get discouraged, but since I am doing almost nothing except a bit here and there with Sarah, I do. I still feel that the gift is there, it is what I should be doing, but there seems to be no real way to get things moving. Yet faith healers get huge crowds. The fruit of self-promotion? Divine backing? What will it take to get this under way? The right time?*

About the time that I had my very brief encounter with the Reverend Canon Mark Pearson, Sarah and I started attending the cathedral of St. James in Chicago, which meant that periodically I came into contact with Bishop Frank Griswold, with whom my former priest had spoken and who had suggested my meeting with Father Sears in the first place. However I had never spoken directly with Bishop Griswold about this matter. As my frustration mounted and absolutely nothing had happened concerning my dreams of doing this work in the church in the two and a half years since the whole thing had begun, I decided to speak with him directly in one last effort to take this matter through proper channels. If nothing came of it then, at least I had spoken with almost everyone I could. Bishop Griswold listened to me with great patience and understanding, and he pointed out that it was a relief for him to deal with this sort of topic, which tends to get lost in the great press of administrative work that a bishop has to face on a daily basis. He said that he had no personal experience in this area and could offer me no direct help, but he did suggest that I talk with a priest in the Church of England who was a healer, Father Robert Llewelyn, former chaplain of the shrine of Julian of Norwich. There was Julian of Norwich again. Because I was already planning to go to England a few months later, I made the arrangements to meet with Father Llewelyn in Norwich.

My encounter with Father Llewelyn in his small flat not far from the shrine was a brief but wonderful experience. He seemed to be surrounded with an aura of gentleness, peace and holiness, and I felt as if I were truly in the presence of a living saint. The time that we spent meditating together was marvelous, and I seemed to slip into a deep meditative state very easily. Despite the exhilarating meeting, Father Llewelyn admitted that, as I was in America and he was in England, there really was little that he could do to help me, and I returned home delighted with having had the opportunity to meet Father Llewelyn, but just as bereft of guidance as I had been before.

I was finally fed up with the frustration and difficulties, whether due to my own weaknesses or to the dark forces that Father Sears had warned me about, and I decided to give up the search for a guru as well as my attempt to use the healing within the church. For two years I simply did work on family members as problems came up and on a few friends. My journal has not a single entry concerning healing for one of those years. During that time, without being conscious of it, I was incorporating a sane philosophy of healing into my life. I was no longer so driven to get on with the healing work and I became more relaxed about it. I really came to believe that physical healing is not as important as development of one's spiritual life and I came to be less concerned with the results of my work. If healing happened, that was fine, and if no apparent healing occurred, that was fine, too, for neither result had much to do with me. I think that it was important for me to learn to detach myself from the results and especially from thinking that the healing was connected to me, for I merely act as a channel for the energy. I came to see that there is indeed a considerable risk of ego in doing this work, just as Father Sears had warned.

The healing work had also taught me to live with considerable ambiguity in life. I can't explain what it is that happens, for it is still a mystery to me. There still are times when there is a result so dramatic that I am stunned and I feel very strange, wanting to give up the healing work and never try it again. Sometimes it even weirds me out. Certainly I can't explain why it came to me. I don't know if healing will happen on any particular occasion and I can't explain why sometimes it happens and sometimes it doesn't. I just wave my hands around and most of the time there are noticeable, positive results.

In the end I came to trust what my hands felt and to rely on a method that I had worked out based on the books that I had read and my own experiences. A friend of mine had been telling me not to look to others as guides but rather to rely on my own inner guide and, in the end, that seems to have happened.

The healing work began to resume with more

intensity when I met Chris, a woman who had received formal training in this sort of healing. We began to do general healing work on each other and then, because she seemed to know so many people with physical problems, we began working together in doing healing work on other people. Within the next two years I came to know other people with considerable experience in healing work. I met Dr. Mary Sinclair, a fellow faculty member at my university who is also a certified practitioner of Healing Touch (HT), a technique that is very similar to Therapeutic Touch or Reiki. For several months we exchanged treatments, during which I gained valuable insight into the technique used by well trained HT practitioners and I also gained a dear friend.

Through another friend I got the name of a healer in Scotland, whom I then went to visit a few months later. It was a pleasure meeting Nan Glen in Falkirk and her own mentor George Geddes. From them I learned of the National Federation of Spiritual Healers in Britain (now called the Healing Trust, I believe) and of the intensive formal training that they had received. I was also able to ask them some of the basic questions that had been plaguing me for years, such as why does the healing work time and time again and then simply not work, and what do they think about while they are doing the work (should I be praying and meditating, or pushing in energy and pulling out pain)? George told me that the first question could not be answered, for the man under whom he had studied, a man who had been doing healing work for forty years, had asked the same question. On the second question, George told me that in his mind he is playing a round of golf on his favorite course while he moves his hands around the person he is working on.

***

By the late 1990s life seemed to have stabilized. Sarah and I were settled down at Grace Episcopal Church and my strange pastime was accepted there. In fact, most of the people I worked on were friends from Grace. I had been doing healing work for six or seven years in different forms, directly on a person with hands above the body and also doing the work at a distance. I had picked up considerable experience and my own understanding and techniques had evolved. I did this healing work on a small scale, working with friends and the occasional person referred to me by friends. I was comfortable with what I was doing, feeling that I could take or leave the healing work, as things worked out. So naturally things had to change.

CHAPTER 8

Going Public

As the twenty-first century began, the three aspects of my life that had developed in the aftermath of the illness that I had in London in 1988, the NDE, my interest in mysticism and the healing work that I was doing began to be intertwined and to be brought out into the open more fully than I could have imagined. My book *Mystics of the Christian Tradition* was published in 2001 and sold well, being used as a textbook in many college and university courses. The appearance of the book meant that if someone were to do an internet search on mystics, my name and book would appear rather prominently. I soon was reviewing books on mysticism for publishers and for scholarly journals, participating in panel discussions on mysticism and giving talks on various aspects of mysticism to groups in the Chicago area.

One of my favorite series of talks that I gave on mysticism was at my own church, Grace Episcopal Church in Oak Park. We had started sponsoring weekend forums given by prominent New Testament scholars like John Dominic Crosson and Marcus Borg, and with the publication of my book I was invited also to give a series of talks on two aspects that I had written about, on Jesus as a mystic and the mystical nature of the early Christian church. That forum was then the inspiration for my friend Mary Lee Bergeron, now a deacon in the Episcopal Church, to organize a weekend of talks on mysticism and healing that was sponsored by the Episcopal Cathedral of St. John in Knoxville, Tennessee. One of my activities was leading a workshop that focused on doing distant healing work, especially relating to healing prayer circles at churches. This was my first official effort at teaching on healing and, to my great relief, I found that the years of reading on healing and practicing healing work had given me the knowledge and experience to help others who wanted to develop this aspect of their lives.

At the same time, I was talking about my NDE. I felt a profound sense of gratitude for the NDE itself as well as for the healing from the paralysis and that I did honor to those experiences by talking about them to those who were truly interested. At first I just spoke about them informally to friends. My first more public discussions about them were to Neal's philosophy classes. Even though I had stopped talking to those classes about my NDE, I told Neal that I would always be willing to meet with individual students who seemed particularly interested in the subject. Through Neal I met Diane Willis, the facilitator of the Chicago Chapter of IANDS (International Association for Near Death Studies), which led to an invitation for me to appear as the featured speaker at one of the chapter's monthly meetings. This was fun for me, for those in attendance were very knowledgeable about NDEs and keenly interested in finding out about my experiences.

My talk to the local IANDS group then led to my

giving a talk at the national IANDS conference in 2004, focusing on the life review aspect of my NDE. This was the largest audience to which I had ever spoken about this very personal and, for me, humiliating part of what I had experienced in London. But I find that people are powerfully moved by the idea of actually experiencing the effects that we have upon the people in our lives.

My connection with the Diane Willis and the Chicago chapter of IANDS also made possible the most public airing of my NDE imaginable, talking about it on a nationally televised program, the *Dr. Oz Show* in 2011. As I understood it, a patient of his had an NDE and discussed it with him, which caused Dr. Oz to become interested in the topic. His production staff contacted the Chicago chapter of IANDS to find possible guests on the show and Diane gave them my name. After a phone interview I was accepted for the program. I had some qualms about the appearance, worried about the consequences of having my experience receive such a public airing. Was I really ready to fly so far above the radar? But I need not have worried. In my segment of the show only my first name was used and no background information about me was given. I was just Steve and I heard from only one friend who happened to be watching Dr. Oz and recognized me.

The NDE, mysticism and healing all came together in 2003 when I met Caroline Myss, the best-selling author and prominent speaker. I had read her book *Anatomy of the Spirit*, which had been given to me by my friend Elaine Mullen in Calgary, Alberta, whom I had met at a professional conference in Warwick, England, in 1997, but it came as quite a surprise that Caroline was living in Oak

Park and had gotten to know my good friends Charles and Sue Wells. Because of her strong interest in mysticism and healing, they had told her about me and she was interested in meeting me. A few months later a speaker at one of her workshops had to cancel at the last minute and Caroline asked if I would fill in for him and give a talk which focused on the NDE, my own healing from paralysis and the healing work that I did. Caroline was teaching on *Sacred Contracts*, which is based on the idea of archetypes and she wanted me to represent the archetype of the Wounded Healer.

Over the next few years I gave a number of talks on mysticism and healing at Caroline's workshops, for this coincided with the focus of her next books, *Entering the Castle* and *Defy Gravity*. I was very comfortable lecturing on mysticism, for I had been doing that at the university for many years. But teaching on healing was a more frightening prospect. After all, I had never received any formal instruction in healing, I had just stumbled my way through, trying this and that, attempting to respond to what my hands were telling me. I couldn't offer the security of a known and respected system of healing like Reiki or Healing Touch, but I did have more than a decade of experiences to draw upon. My keeping a written record of all the work that I had done proved to be an extremely valuable resource.

The core of my teaching is not to get locked into the requirements and procedures of any particular system of healing but rather to experiment and come to trust the information that is being provided by your hands. Inevitably I was asked what my system of healing is called, so I borrowed rather shamelessly from the martial arts system of Bruce Lee. He felt that existing schools of martial arts were too rigid in insisting that one technique be followed in every instance, arguing that adaptability to changing circumstances are more successful. I jokingly summarized the essentials of his teaching (which happened to be the same as mine, a nice coincidence) as RARA—**R**esearch your own experience; **A**dopt what seems right to you; **R**eject what doesn't seem useful; **A**dd from your own experiences. With full acknowledgment in my talks of my debt to Bruce Lee I borrowed the name that he gave his system—Jeet Kune Do, "the Way of the Intercepting Fist"—to give my own experimental system a classy and exotic sounding name. As scary as I found it at times to teach on healing, at the same time it felt very right to me, as if it were what I am really supposed to be doing. It felt frighteningly right to do it.

After several years of this somewhat sporadic teaching on healing, Caroline, who was by then working on her book *Defy Gravity*, suggested that the two of us hold a special weekend workshop dedicated to the subject of healing, with me giving four talks. I was both very excited about the idea of spending an entire weekend dedicated to healing work, but also I was deeply afraid of it. It was one thing to give one talk at one of Caroline's workshops, for there were other speakers as well as Caroline's dynamic presence, so I didn't feel a lot of pressure. If I were to fall on my face there would be many other presentations to compensate. But now I would be featured along with Caroline and I had never tried giving so many talks in a single workshop before. Falling on my face at this venue would be highly embarrassing. But I still felt deep inside of me that this is what I am supposed to be doing and I felt highly honored that Caroline would want to do such a workshop with me. Besides, I knew that those who came to the workshop were really there to hear Caroline and not me, which alleviated much of my anxiety.

I need not have worried, the workshop was a great success and we repeated it three more times. I grew more comfortable as my teaching seemed to be well received, so comfortable that in time I gave a healing workshop on my own, without the security of having Caroline as the headliner. I met Yola Dunne at one of Caroline's workshops and we became good friends. Yola asked if I would give a workshop on healing in the Canadian town where she lives, Chelsea, Québec, which she would organize. All I had to do was to show up, so of course I agreed. I thought a small scale, one-day workshop would be a good test to determine if I would be able to go solo. As with the workshops that I had done with Caroline, this workshop seemed to be well received, giving me encouragement to give more workshops teaching about healing in the future.

There were some distractions during this period. Most importantly Sarah and I divorced after seventeen years of marriage. Having an NDE is no guarantee that life will go smoothly or that all of one's decisions are wise ones. In the end, we remain what the Being in The Beyond said to me, we are human, with all the positive and negative aspects of that existence.

Over the years I learned that an NDE is a constantly unfolding experience, not something that happens once, is then over and then you get on with your life. You never know where it will lead, what changes it will bring about in your life. When I went off to attend the conference in London in June of 1988 in a lost state of mind, I had no inkling of how close to death I would come, of the paralysis that I would face, of how my survival would force such changes in my life. I had no idea of the adventures in healing that awaited me.

In addition, Near Death Experiences tend to come when one is near death. At times a number of difficult health problems remain after the NDE is over. In these cases, people have to work on rehabilitating their bodies in addition to trying to assimilate the "lessons from the light" into their lives. It may be an open question as to which is more difficult, physical rehabilitation or psychological and spiritual rehabilitation.

In such cases, the NDE is an earthquake that turns one inside out, demolishing one's basic understanding of God, self, life and the universe. The tremors and aftershocks continue on for years afterwards in the effort to integrate the lessons learned from the experience into life in this world. Moreover, people who have these experiences often find their own lives changed in ways that would have been unimaginable to them before the earthquake hit.

In this sense, an NDE can be much more than up the tunnel, into the paradise, and back into this world again. In such cases, the NDE is only the beginning of a long, difficult and challenging process of remaking one's very existence. Seen this way, what is commonly taken for an NDE only initiates the true, continuing Near Death Experience. After the return from what is beyond, the first and inescapable question is, "Now what?"

Made in the USA
Lexington, KY
16 June 2017